THE VALUE OF TIME IN PASSENGER TRANSPORTATION:
THE DEMAND FOR AIR TRAVEL

THE VALUE OF TIME

IN PASSENGER TRANSPORTATION:

THE DEMAND FOR AIR TRAVEL

REUBEN GRONAU

The Hebrew University of Jerusalem

 OCCASIONAL PAPER 109

NATIONAL BUREAU OF ECONOMIC RESEARCH

New York   1970

Distributed by Columbia University Press

New York and London

RELATION OF THE DIRECTORS TO THE WORK AND PUBLICATIONS OF THE NATIONAL BUREAU OF ECONOMIC RESEARCH

1. The object of the National Bureau of Economic Research is to ascertain and to present to the public important economic facts and their interpretation in a scientific and impartial manner. The Board of Directors is charged with the responsibility of ensuring that the work of the National Bureau is carried on in strict conformity with this object.

2. The President of the National Bureau shall submit to the Board of Directors, or to its Executive Committee, for their formal adoption all specific proposals for research to be instituted.

3. No research report shall be published until the President shall have submitted to each member of the Board the manuscript proposed for publication, and such information as will, in his opinion and in the opinion of the author, serve to determine the suitability of the report for publication in accordance with the principles of the National Bureau. Each manuscript shall contain a summary drawing attention to the nature and treatment of the problem studied, the character of the data and their utilization in the report, and the main conclusions reached.

4. For each manuscript so submitted, a special committee of the Board shall be appointed by majority agreement of the President and Vice Presidents (or by the Executive Committee in case of inability to decide on the part of the President and Vice Presidents), consisting of three directors selected as nearly as may be one from each general division of the Board. The names of the special manuscript committee shall be stated to each Director when the manuscript is submitted to him. It shall be the duty of each member of the special manuscript committee to read the manuscript. If each member of the manuscript committee signifies his approval within thirty days of the transmittal of the manuscript, the report may be published. If at the end of that period any member of the manuscript committee withholds his approval, the President shall then notify each member of the Board, requesting approval or disapproval of publication, and thirty days additional shall be granted for this purpose. The manuscript shall then not be published unless at least a majority of the entire Board who shall have voted on the proposal within the time fixed for the receipt of votes shall have approved.

5. No manuscript may be published, though approved by each member of the special manuscript committee, until forty-five days have elapsed from the transmittal of the report in manuscript form. The interval is allowed for the receipt of any memorandum of dissent or reservation, together with a brief statement of his reasons, that any member may wish to express; and such memorandum of dissent or reservation shall be published with the manuscript if he so desires. Publication does not, however, imply that each member of the Board has read the manuscript, or that either members of the Board in general or the special committee have passed on its validity in every detail.

6. Publications of the National Bureau issued for informational purposes concerning the work of the Bureau and its staff, or issued to inform the public of activities of Bureau staff, and volumes issued as a result of various conferences involving the National Bureau shall contain a specific disclaimer noting that such publication has not passed through the normal review procedures required in this resolution. The Executive Committee of the Board is charged with review of all such publications from time to time to ensure that they do not take on the character of formal research reports of the National Bureau, requiring formal Board approval.

7. Unless otherwise determined by the Board or exempted by the terms of paragraph 6, a copy of this resolution shall be printed in each National Bureau publication.

(Resolution adopted October 25, 1926, and revised February 6, 1933,
February 24, 1941, and April 20, 1968)

CONTENTS

TABLES

CHARTS

PREFACE

THIS PAPER by Reuben Gronau has its origins in two streams of work at the National Bureau of Economic Research. On the theoretical side, Gary S. Becker has fashioned a simple and powerful analytical apparatus to deal with the inescapable constraints faced by every individual in the use of time. No matter how high income rises, no matter how rapidly productivity grows, no matter how abundant natural and man-made resources become, each person has available to him a maximum of twenty-four hours in a day, seven days in a week. Starting with this fact, Becker has shown how insights concerning the price of time, the time intensity of various activities, and the substitution possibilities between time and goods and services can illuminate numerous aspects of economic behavior.

Perhaps nowhere is this more relevant than in studying the service industries, an activity which my associates and I have been engaged in for several years. Many of the most important services, such as medical care, education, and personal care, are extremely time intensive; frequently the most valuable input into the production process is the time of the consumer. Other services, such as maintenance and repair, laundry and dry cleaning, domestic servants, and some aspects of banking, are demanded in part because they save time for the purchaser. In our studies of productivity in retailing and personal services, in our attempt to understand the demand for medical care, and in many other phases of our project, we have found ourselves asking what it is that determines the price of time, and how do people take this price into account in making economic decisions.

Reuben Gronau has attempted to answer such questions in one well-defined economic area: passenger demand for air transportation. By developing and applying Becker's model, and by utilizing data made available to the National Bureau of Economic Research by the Port of New York Authority, he has obtained some highly interesting empirical results.

The first important substantive finding concerns the way the price of time affects the choice between air transportation and other modes of travel. Given the distance traveled, and the price of time, a theoretical model predicts the logical passenger choice among air, rail, and bus transportation. These predictions conform well to actual experience, as is shown in Chapter 4.

A second finding, more tentative than the first, indicates that business travelers behave as if their price of time is approximately equal to their hourly earnings; the price of time of personal travelers appears to be considerably lower (see Chapter 5). In the course of reaching this conclusion, Gronau estimates income and price elasticities of demand for air travel and provides new information on the relation between family income and hourly earnings. To be sure, the value of time to an individual may vary not only with the purpose of the trip, but may also vary with its length, time of day, and other factors. Moreover, the value of time saved in travel may be different for different individuals even when hourly earnings are identical. Thus, the application of Gronau's techniques and estimates to specific problems requires additional empirical information relevant to the particular problem under study.

In the final chapter, which may be of greatest interest to the general reader, the author illustrates how estimates of the price of time could be applied to several problems currently facing policy makers in the transportation field. He discusses the possible impact of the supersonic passenger plane on the demand for air travel, and the possible impact of faster trains on the demand for bus, train, and air transportation.

The problem attacked in this book is complex and controversial; the limitations of the data and of the econometric techniques should be fully recognized. Moreover, the applications of the findings are plainly labeled as illustrative. The study does, however, provide significant support for the conventional wisdom that "time is money" and does so within a theoretical framework that should stimulate and facilitate further research on this important determinant of human behavior.

VICTOR R. FUCHS
VICE-PRESIDENT-RESEARCH

ACKNOWLEDGMENTS

THIS BOOK is based on my Ph.D. dissertation prepared at Columbia University in 1965–67. The subject was suggested to me by Gary Becker as an outgrowth of his study of the allocation of time. Having established the point of departure Becker continued to advise me throughout, especially with regard to the final exposition and the discussion of the empirical results. More important than his specific contributions, however, is the opportunity I had to work with him, for which I am grateful.

Many people at the National Bureau have been most helpful in reviewing drafts of the study and in advising on specific questions. They include Victor Fuchs, who in addition to advice generously provided me with encouragement; Jacob Mincer, who made several apt suggestions and gave me several good leads; Stanley Diller, whose help was invaluable in writing the first drafts; John R. Meyer and Gerald Kraft, whose extensive comments proved crucial for the shaping of the final draft; and the Directors' Reading Committee, consisting of Emilio G. Collado, Maurice W. Lee, and George Cline Smith.

I am also grateful to Lorraine Catarcio, Rose Ferro, and Roberta B. Watson, who showed super human patience typing the formula-burdened text; to H. Irving Foreman, who drew the graphs; and to Virginia Meltzer, who edited the text.

Sam Brown of the Civil Aeronautics Board and Fred Hurst of the New York Port Authority were most helpful in providing me with the necessary data.

Work on this study was supported in part by a grant from the Ford Foundation for the National Bureau's study of the service industries.

A grant of computer time from the International Business Machines Corporation is also gratefully acknowledged.

Certain data used in this book were derived by the author from punched cards furnished under a joint project sponsored by the U.S. Bureau of the Census and the Population Council and containing selected 1960 Census information for a 0.1 per cent sample of the population of the United States. Neither the Census Bureau nor the Population Council assumes any responsibility for the validity of any of the figures or interpretations of the figures published herein based on this material.

REUBEN GRONAU

ONE

Introduction and Summary of Results

IN PASSENGER TRANSPORTATION, the consumer desires the greatest possible speed and comfort, as well as other factors, at the lowest possible price, and the history of the industry is one of progressive improvements in these relationships. This book considers consumer preferences as they are influenced by the relationship of speed (or time) and price. The latest manifestations of technological improvements in regard to time are the proposed 300 mile-per-hour trains, the 1,800 mph supersonic transport planes (SST), the short-take-off and -landing planes (STOL), and the vertical-take-off and -landing planes (VTOL). Since the social benefit of these innovations as well as their profitability depends, in part at least, on the value placed by the community on time saving, a study of consumer attitudes toward time in relation to cost should be useful.

Until quite recently, economic literature had little to say about the value of time saving innovations to the individual consumer or to the community as a whole. Social welfare problems relating to the supply of transportation services (e.g., the effect of regulation) drew the focus of attention away from the *demand* factors. Regulators were given only meager information on the travelers' sensitivity to changes in the trip's price, a crucial variable in any pricing policy.[1] In none of the studies did traveling time play any role.

---

[1] Richard Caves mentions only two studies made prior to 1962 relating to the demand elasticity in his *Air Transport and Its Regulators*, Cambridge, Massachusetts, 1962, pp. 31–54.

In the sixties there has been an awakening of interest in the demand for transportation resulting from the fast expansion of the air industry and increased pressure on the federal government to coordinate the transportation market. The increasing number of studies in this field has brought to the fore the effect of traveling time on consumer preference for modes of travel. However, most of these studies lack an explicit theoretical exposition; time is usually treated as a variable affecting tastes.

These studies discuss time in relation to utility and comfort. The utility a traveler derives from a trip is directly related to the amount of traveling time involved and the discomfort of traveling increases with traveling time. Therefore, this approach holds, differences in traveling time by different modes of transportation serving the same route are reflected in the differences in the utilities these modes yield. The train is usually faster than the automotive modes (bus and private car), and air is usually faster than ground transportation. Hence, the observed shift of travelers from bus to train to air as their incomes rise is interpreted as analogous to a shift to better housing, better food, etc. Since differences in traveling time between the various modes increase with the distance of the trip, as do the differences in utilities, the air carriers' superiority increases with distance and makes them the dominant mode of transportation for long-range trips.

This explanation, which ties the choice of a mode of travel to the amount of discomfort involved in traveling, may have a certain intuitive appeal but is lacking in analytical power. Its major handicap is reliance on a cardinal concept of utility, i.e., on the notion that utility is a measurable entity. This explanation assumes that one can compare the utilities derived by different individuals from different commodities. It can be used, therefore, as an operative tool of analysis only if the utilities derived from trips by different modes of transportation are measurable. For only if the relationship between traveling time and utility can be defined in quantitative terms can one predict the effect of a reduction in traveling time on the demand for travel.

A more promising approach treats elapsed time as one of the factors affecting the price of a trip, rather than its utility. Time is a scarce resource and, as such, commands a positive price. This fact has been long recognized by economists concerned with problems of production.

It was suggested recently that the same approach applies to problems of consumption.[2] Consumption, according to this argument, involves the combination of goods purchased in the market and the time provided by the consumer. The price of any consumption activity depends on the price of the goods involved and the value the consumer places on his time. A trip from New York to Boston by plane involves a monetary cost of $16 and 3 hours of traveling.[3] The cost of the trip to a passenger who assigns to his time a value of $5 an hour adds up, therefore, to $31.

The value placed on time increases with the household's income. This relationship is reflected both in differences in the consumption patterns of households with different incomes, and in the ratio of time to market goods used by each for its consumption activities. The higher the consumer's price of time, the smaller his tendency to use time-intensive activities, i.e., activities that contain a large time component. For example, if the trip from New York to Boston by bus involves a monetary cost of $8 and 5 hours of traveling, a traveler whose price of time is $3 an hour will go by bus (the total costs being $23 by bus vs. $25 by air) while a traveler whose price of time is $5 an hour will find it cheaper to use the faster (less time-intensive) mode, namely air (the costs being $31 for air vs. $33 for bus).

The time intensity of a trip (i.e., the part that time constitutes in the total cost of the trip) depends, among other things, on the distance traveled. Both differences in fare and in time elapsed between air and ground transportation increase with distance. However, the time differential increases faster than the fare differential resulting in an increased tendency to shift to a faster mode as the distance increases. For example, a bus trip from New York to Chicago involves a monetary cost of $28 and 17 hours of traveling, while the same trip by air costs $49 but lasts only 5 hours. A traveler whose price of time is $3 an hour who, as has been shown, found it cheaper to go to Boston by bus, prefers to go to Chicago by air (the cost being $64 for air vs. $79 for bus).

[2] See Gary S. Becker's "A Theory of the Allocation of Time," *Economic Journal,* September 1965, and Jacob Mincer's "Market Prices, Opportunity Costs, and Income Effects" in *Measurement in Economics: Studies in Mathematical Economics and Econometrics in Memory of Yehuda Grunfeld,* C. F. Christ, ed., Stanford, California, 1963.

[3] In this study, travel time is that necessary to go from one central urban area to the other.

The competition between private and public modes of transportation is dominated by the insensitivity of the monetary costs of a trip by private car to changes in the number of the people going on the trip. Thus, if the money cost of traveling by car from New York to Boston is $14 and the elapsed time 5 hours, an individual whose price of time is $5 an hour will prefer air to car when he is traveling alone (the total costs being $31 and $39, respectively), but if he is accompanied by another two people with the same price of time he will use his car rather than go by air (the costs being $89 and $93, respectively).

The price of time of children is relatively low and, thus, the inclusion of children in the party may weigh heavily in favor of the car. For example, two persons going to Boston whose price of time is $5 an hour may use air transportation rather than their private car (the cost of the former being $62 vs. $64 for the latter). On the other hand, if one of this party is a child whose price of time is zero, the party will go by car (the cost being $39) rather than air ($47).

The price of time becomes, therefore, a crucial determinant of the choice of mode. A theory that regards time as one of the factors determining the price of the trip provides us with a strong tool for the analysis of existing traffic patterns. However, to make this tool an instrument for the prediction of future demand one has to specify the exact form of the relationship between the price of time and income. Economic theory states only that this price is an increasing function of income. It does not indicate, however, whether the value of time changes at a faster or a slower rate than the traveler's earnings, whether it depends on the amount of time involved, or whether it is affected by the mode used. The estimation of the exact relationship is an empirical problem.

Scarcity of data confined the empirical work to one case study— passenger demand for air transportation. Interview data were used to estimate separately business travelers' and personal travelers' price of time and demand for air trips. Assuming that the price of time is proportional to hourly earnings and independent of the time and mode of travel, it was found that business travelers value their time at about their hourly earnings. In other words, employers tend to view traveling time as working time lost and, hence, assign to their employees' time a value that equals the foregone output.

One would expect the same relationship between the price of time and hourly earnings to apply to personal travel, if the traveler is free to change his working time at will. But usually this is not the case. In the short run at least, such an employee is bound by some institutional arrangement: number of daily working hours, number of days worked per week, etc. When traveling for personal purposes, therefore, he may not assign to his time a value that equals his hourly take-home pay. Unfortunately, we cannot determine the exact nature of this relationship; the data do not show any systematic relationship between the imputed value of time and hourly earnings or annual income.

Both estimates of the relationship between the price of time and hourly earnings have to be approached with care. For one, these estimates are subject to random sampling errors, thus also admitting some alternative interpretations. Moreover, our estimates may depend on the assumption that the value travelers place on their time is proportional to their hourly earnings. The verification of this assumption calls for additional investigation.

A by-product of the evaluation of the price of time is the estimate of the demand function for air travel. Income has been found to be the major variable determining demand. The household's number of trips is very sensitive to changes in its income. One would expect an increase in income to lead to a greater proportionate expansion in air travel, since income elasticities are significantly greater than one.

A major policy problem is whether a fare cut would result in an increase or a decrease in air-carriers' revenues; in other words, whether a reduction in fares would lead to a greater or a smaller proportional increase in air travel. In this study, the price of the trip is defined as a combination of both money and time costs. The effect of a price change on the demand for trips is examined but there is no attempt to isolate the effect of changes in the pecuniary component (i.e., fares) on this demand. Still, the study provides some indirect answers to this highly disputed question.

It is found that any price reduction would lead to a smaller proportional increase of both personal and business travel. In other words, the price elasticities of both the demand for personal air travel and the demand for business air travel are smaller than one (however, the difference in the latter case is not statistically significant). Since any cut in fares leads to a smaller proportional reduction of total price, these results support the notion that a reduction of fares would be accompanied by a fall in air-carriers' revenues.

Finally, it is argued that business air travelers are more sensitive to changes in income and price than personal travelers. Both income and price elasticities of business travelers exceed, in their absolute value, those of personal travelers. This result may seem somewhat puzzling when viewed against the background of the air-carriers' promotion policies (e.g., excursion fares, family plans, etc.), which seem to be aimed primarily at the personal traveler.

Hypothetical illustrations related to the supersonic transport plane and to the high speed train demonstrate that the value travelers place on their time is crucial in determining the future modal split. Admittedly, the estimates provided in this study can be regarded only as preliminary evidence that must be substantiated by future research. A major handicap in this is the scarcity of data.

The transition period from piston to jet passenger planes furnished an ideal testing ground for our theory. Given information on motives and socioeconomic characteristics of passengers on both the slower and faster equipment one would have been able to derive some more reliable estimates of the price of time. This opportunity has been missed. Fortunately, economists may have a second chance. The introduction of faster planes and trains should yield almost perfect conditions for a controlled experiment to answer the elusive question of how people value their time. It is of utmost importance that this opportunity should not be missed.

Chapter 2 opens the study with a short discussion of the factors determining the price of time. Chapter 3 analyzes the variables shaping the demand for trips and the modal split. Noting the limitations of the theory attributing this choice to the discomfort of travel, Chapter 4 shows that the theory of the allocation of time goes a long way in explaining the structure of the transportation market. A discussion of the statistical method and the nature of the data prepares the stage for estimation of the demand for air transportation and the price of time in Chapter 5. Chapter 6 closes the report with some applications of our model to some current problems—the supersonic passenger plane and the fast trains.

TWO

The VALUE OF TIME

"TIME IS MONEY" is a frequently used adage. Economists, recognizing the effect of time on the production process, have incorporated this effect in the distinction between a firm's short-run and long-run costs. It can be shown, however, that time exerts a somewhat similar effect on household consumption decisions. In effect, a household can be regarded as a producer of activities, combining its own time with market goods and services:

$$Z_i = f_i(X_i, T_i), \qquad i = 1, \ldots, n, \tag{2.1}$$

where Z_i denotes the ith activity, X_i the market inputs, and T_i the time involved. The activity, a "visit," for example, is produced by combining transportation, hotel and restaurant services, traveling time, and time spent at the point of destination.

Different units of time may vary in their productive capacity. For example, daytime may be more efficient for the production of a business visit, while nighttime may be more efficient for producing a visit to friends and relatives; wintertime may be more efficient for producing a visit to Florida, and summertime may be more efficient for producing a visit to Yellowstone National Park.

The production process is subject to two constraints: the budget constraint determines the total expenditures on the market inputs; and the time constraint determines the total expenditures of time inputs. Specifically,

$$\sum_{i=1}^{n} P_i X_i = Y, \qquad \sum_{i=1}^{n} T_i = T_0, \tag{2.2}$$

where P_i denotes the price of the market input in activity i, Y is income, and T_0 is the total time available for consumption activities. The household's aim is to maximize its utility (U),

$$U = U(Z_1, \ldots, Z_n), \tag{2.3}$$

subject to the above constraints.

The necessary conditions for an optimum are satisfied when

$$u_i = \lambda(P_i x_i + \frac{\mu}{\lambda} t_i) \qquad i = 1, \ldots, n, \tag{2.4}$$

where $u_i = \dfrac{\partial U}{\partial Z_i}$ denotes the marginal utility of activity i, λ is the marginal utility of income, μ is the marginal utility of time, and $x_i = \dfrac{\partial X_i}{\partial Z_i}$ and $t_i = \dfrac{\partial T_i}{\partial Z_i}$ are the marginal inputs of market goods and time, respectively.[1]

The optimal combination of inputs in the production of any activity is attained when the ratio of the marginal products of time and market goods equals their relative prices,

$$\frac{\partial Z_i / \partial T_i}{\partial Z_i / \partial X_i} = \frac{x_i}{t_i} = \frac{\mu / \lambda}{P_i} = \frac{K}{P_i}, \tag{2.5}$$

where $K = \dfrac{\mu}{\lambda}$ is the (shadow) price of time.[2] The total price of activity i

---

[1]The equilibrium condition (2.4) is obtained by maximizing equation (2.3) subject to the constraints of equation (2.2). Using the Lagrange method,

$$L = U(Z_1, \ldots, Z_n) + \lambda(Y - \Sigma P_i X_i) + \mu(T_0 - \Sigma T_i). \tag{1}$$

The necessary conditions for a maximum are

$$\frac{\partial L}{\partial Z_i} = \frac{\partial U}{\partial Z_i} - \lambda P_i \frac{\partial X_i}{\partial Z_i} - \mu \frac{\partial T_i}{\partial Z_i} = u_i - \lambda P_i x_i - \mu t_i = 0, \tag{2}$$

that is, $u_i = \lambda P_i x_i + \mu t_i$.

[2]Maximizing equation (1) from note 1 with respect to X_i and T_i yields

$$\frac{\partial L}{\partial X_i} = \frac{\partial U}{\partial Z_i} \frac{\partial Z_i}{\partial X_i} - \lambda P_i = \frac{u_i}{x_i} - \lambda P_i = 0, \text{ that is, } u_i = \lambda P_i x_i, \tag{3}$$

and

$$\frac{\partial L}{\partial T_i} = \frac{\partial U}{\partial Z_i} \frac{\partial Z_i}{\partial T_i} - \mu = \frac{u_i}{t_i} - \mu = 0, \text{ that is, } u_i = \mu t_i. \tag{4}$$

Dividing (4) by (3) yields the equilibrium condition (2.5).

(Π_i) equals its marginal cost of production and consists of two parts, the money component and the time component

$$\Pi_i = P_i x_i + K t_i. \tag{2.6}$$

Equation (2.4) can be written in the familiar form

$$u_i = \lambda \Pi_i. \tag{2.7}$$

The price of time (K) depends on the household's tastes, its production functions, its income, and the total consumption time that stands at its disposal. When the production functions are linear homogeneous, the price of time becomes a sole function of the household's tastes and factor scarcity (Y/T_0). An increase in income results in an increase in the intrinsic price of time, a shift in production toward goods, and a shift in consumption toward goods-intensive activities.[3] The share of goods-intensive activities in the household's optimal activity "basket" is bound to increase, unless these activities are associated with very low income elasticities.

Up to now we have assumed that the amount of work supplied by the household is exogenously determined. The number of daily working hours, the length of the work week, and the length of vacations are given at least in the short run. The amount of consumption time, this argument goes, is outside the household's realm of decisions. This assumption proves to be too restrictive when the household's long-run decisions are analyzed. Assuming that the household can change the amount of work it offers in the market (Z_w), the constraints confronting the production process and the household's objective function must be redefined. The household aims at maximizing its utility function,

$$U = U(Z_1, \ldots, Z_n, Z_w), \tag{2.8}$$

subject to an endogenous budget constraint,

$$\sum_{i=1}^{n} P_i X_i + P_w X_w = W(Z_w) + V = Y(Z_w), \tag{2.9}$$

and an exogenous time constraint,

[3] See T. M. Rybczynski, "Factor Endowment and Relative Commodity Prices," *Economica*, November 1955, for the application of a similar analysis to the field of international trade.

$$\sum_{i=1}^{n} T_i + T_w = T_0', \tag{2.10}$$

where $W(Z_w)$ denotes earning, V other income, and T_0' is the total time available (e.g., 24 hours a day, 168 hours a week). The optimal supply of work is determined by the equation

$$u_w = \mu t_w - \lambda w, \tag{2.11}$$

where $w = \dfrac{\partial W(Z_w)}{\partial Z_w} - P_w x_w$ is the net marginal wage rate (i.e., the household's remuneration for the marginal unit of work it sells in the market minus any money costs incurred).[4] Measuring the activity "work" (Z_w) in terms of its time inputs (e.g., hours of work) $t_w = 1$, the value of the marginal utility of time is $\mu = \lambda w + u_w$ and the price of time equals the sum of the marginal wage rate and the money equivalent of the marginal utility of work

$$K = \frac{\mu}{\lambda} = w + \frac{u_w}{\lambda}. \tag{2.12}$$

Equations (2.5), (2.6), and (2.7) describe the necessary optimum conditions for production and consumption. The price of time is determined by the net marginal wage rate, by the household's taste for work, and by the marginal utility of income. Only when work does not involve any utility or disutility ($u_w = 0$) does the price of time equal the marginal wage rate. In general, it may either exceed it, if the psychic income is sufficiently large ($u_w > 0$), or be smaller, when work involves marginal disutilities ($u_w < 0$). If $u_w \neq 0$, the price of time may change even if the marginal wage rate is constant, since a change in income or a change in the taste for work may change u_w/λ.

[4] Let

$$L = U(Z_1, \ldots, Z_n, Z_w) + \lambda[W(Z_w) + V - (\Sigma P_i X_i + P_w X_w)]$$
$$+ \mu[T_0' - (\Sigma T_i + T_w)]. \tag{5}$$

Differentiating with respect to Z_w,

$$\frac{\partial L}{\partial Z_w} = \frac{\partial U}{\partial Z_w} + \lambda\left(\frac{\partial W}{\partial Z_w} - P_w \frac{\partial X_w}{\partial Z_w}\right) - \mu \frac{\partial T_w}{\partial Z_w} = u_w + \lambda w - \mu t_w = 0. \tag{6}$$

Any increase in the price of time, whether as a result of a change in the wage rate or of a change in the money equivalent of the marginal utility of work, results in a substitution in production in favor of goods and a substitution in consumption in favor of the goods-intensive activities. The effect of this change on the relative share of the various activities depends on whether it is accompanied by any income effects, and on the direction and magnitude of these effects. An increase of wages, for example, tends to reduce the share of time-intensive activities in the optimal activity combination, unless their income elasticity is substantially greater than unity.

THREE

The Demand for Transportation

TRANSPORTATION SERVICES are market inputs that combine with the traveler's time to produce a trip to a certain destination. An air trip (Z_A), for example, is a combination of the air-carriers' services (X_A) and of elapsed time (T_A)

$$Z_A = f(X_A, T_A). \tag{3.1}$$

Similarly, for a bus trip

$$Z_B = f(X_B, T_B). \tag{3.2}$$

The demand for the various transportation services (X_A, X_B) is a derived demand depending on the demand for air and bus trips. The demand for trips depends, in turn, on the direct utility they yield and on their contribution to the production of a third activity—a visit to the point of destination (Z_v),

$$Z_v = f(X_v, T_v, Z_A, Z_B), \tag{3.3}$$

where X_v is other market inputs involved in the production of the visit (e.g., hotel, restaurant, and transportation services at the point of destination), and T_v is other time inputs involved (i.e., the length of stay).

The activity "visit" is produced for one of two reasons: to yield direct utilities when the visit is for personal purposes, or to serve as an input in the production of market goods when the visit is for business purposes. The demand for personal visits and the demand for business visits reflect the marginal utility and the marginal productivity of the visit, respectively, which depend in turn on the "attractiveness" of the point of destination, i.e., the size, the level of economic activity, and the scenery of the place. Given personal taste, the demand for personal visits is a function of the visit's price, the price of related activities (e.g., visits to other places, other recreation activities, and other forms of communication), and the household's income.

A business trip can be regarded as a short-run migration movement. Ignoring interest rates, the incentive to migrate is inversely related to the costs of migration and directly related to the immigrant's marginal product differential. The demand for business visits depends, therefore, on price factors similar to those affecting the demand for personal visits, and on the difference between the passenger's marginal product at the point of origin and his marginal product at the point of destination. This difference seems, as in other cases of migration, to increase with the passenger's skills and, hence, with his income.

The demand elasticity of a factor of production is directly related to the demand elasticity of the product, the elasticity of substitution in production between the factor and other inputs, and the share of the factor in total costs. Therefore, the demand elasticity of a trip depends, aside from the demand of visits, on the elasticity of substitution between trips and other inputs used in the production of the visit, and on the share of the trip in the visit's costs. The optimal allocation of inputs in the production of a visit calls for

$$\frac{\partial Z_v / \partial Z_i}{\partial Z_v / \partial X_v} = \frac{x_v}{z_i} = \frac{\Pi_i - (u_i/\lambda)}{P_v} = \frac{\Pi_i'}{P_v}$$

$$i = A, B \qquad (3.4)$$

$$\frac{\partial Z_v / \partial Z_i}{\partial Z_v / \partial T_v} = \frac{t_v}{z_i} = \frac{\Pi_i - (u_i/\lambda)}{K} = \frac{\Pi_i'}{K},$$

where $z_i = \dfrac{\partial Z_i}{\partial Z_v}$ is the marginal input of the trip in the production of a visit, t_v and x_v are the marginal inputs of other time and market goods, respectively, P_v is the price of the other market goods, and Π_i' is the trip's total price. The price of the trip consists of the time and money inputs required to produce the trip (Π_i) minus the money equivalent of the marginal utility derived from the trip. An increase in the price of the trip results in a substitution toward the other time and market inputs. Most of these inputs vary directly with the length of the stay. Hence, the higher the price of the trip, the greater is a passenger's tendency to prolong his stay and to cut the number of his trips. On the other hand, the higher the costs of hotels and restaurants and the lower the costs of the trip, the greater is the passenger's tendency to return home quickly. The price of the trip is directly related to its distance, and, thus, one expects the length of stay and the trip's distance to be positively correlated. The ease with which the passenger can increase his length of stay at the expense of the number of trips, and vice versa, directly affects the elasticity of substitution between the trip and the other factors. The share of the trip's costs in the total cost decreases with the length of the stay when this elasticity exceeds unity, and increases when the elasticity is smaller than unity.

Another factor affecting the demand for trips by a given mode is the elasticity of substitution among trips by different modes. The optimum conditions call for the marginal rate of technical substitution between trips by various modes to be equal to their relative prices

$$\frac{\partial Z_v/\partial Z_A}{\partial Z_v/\partial Z_B} = \frac{z_B}{z_A} = \frac{\Pi_A'}{\Pi_B'} = \frac{P_A x_A + K t_A - (u_A/\lambda)}{P_B x_B + K t_B - (u_B/\lambda)}. \tag{3.5}$$

The activities "air-trip" and "bus-trip" are assumed to be perfect substitutes in the production of the visit. Both activities are equally efficient in conveying the passenger from one place to the other; hence, $z_B/z_A = 1$. The modal split is determined, therefore, exclusively by the shape of the price line. This shape reflects the differences among the various modes in the direct utilities (u_i), and in the time intensities $[t_i/(P_i x_i + K t_i)]$. The direct utilities vary among the modes as a function of the convenience, prestige, and risk involved. In a special case, when the marginal utility of one of the modes is sufficiently large, the money equivalent of the marginal utility may exceed the money and time outlays involved in producing the trip, the price of the trip becomes negative, and the passenger will specialize, using only one mode. In general, the price line slopes downward. A stable interior equilibrium is attained at the point of tangency between the concave isocost and the straight isoquant curves. The traveler produces his visits using Z_{A0} air trips and Z_{B0} bus trips (Figure 1).

Changes in the traveler's income and in the distance of the trip affect

FIGURE 1

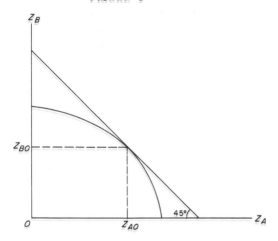

the relative prices and the modal choice by affecting both the trip's costs of production and the money equivalent of the direct utility the trip generates.

The theory of discomfort tries to connect the choice of mode with the direct utilities involved in traveling by the various modes. To isolate the effect of the marginal direct utilities, let us assume that the passenger's price of time equals zero. The relative price of an air trip compared with a bus trip is, in this case,

$$\frac{\Pi'_A}{\Pi'_B} = \frac{P_A x_A - (u_A/\lambda)}{P_B x_B - (u_B/\lambda)}. \tag{3.6}$$

The necessary condition for an interior equilibrium is

$$\frac{\Pi'_A}{\Pi'_B} = 1 = >u_A - u_B = \lambda(P_A x_A - P_B x_B), \tag{3.7}$$

i.e., the money equivalent of the marginal utility differential equals the difference in marginal money outlays per trip. A change in income, which changes the marginal utility of income (λ), affects the slope of the price line and the modal choice. Moreover, the difference between the marginal utilities and the difference between the money outlays may vary with the distance of the trip, resulting in a change in the optimal combination of modes as the distance increases.

Unfortunately, one cannot predict the effect of changes in income and the distance of the trip on the modal split without explicitly specifying (a) the effect of changes in income on the marginal utility of income, and (b) the functional form (g) relating utility with the number of the trips and their distance (M)

$$U_i = g(Z_i, M) \qquad i = A, B. \tag{3.8}$$

These two requirements cannot be satisfied unless one is ready to adopt a cardinal concept of utility. Given the conventional ordinal utility approach, the theory of discomfort can be used only as an *ad hoc* explanation of the transportation market; it is incapable of providing an operative tool of prediction.

To circumvent the difficulties inherent in the theory of discomfort, one has to assume that the trip does not convey any direct marginal utility ($u_i = 0$). This assumption is followed throughout the rest of this study.

The price of a trip was defined in equation (3.4) as the sum of the time and money inputs required to produce the trip (Π_i) plus the money equivalent of the direct marginal utility. Given our simplifying assumption, this last term equals zero. Moreover, when the production of a trip by mode i requires a fixed money input P_i and a fixed time component T_i (i.e., when the marginal inputs of market goods and time are constant and equal $x_i = 1$ and $t_i = T_i$, respectively), the price of the trip is

$$\Pi_i = P_i + KT_i. \tag{3.9}$$

This price is invariant to the level of activity Z_i. The concave isocost curve in Figure 1 can, therefore, be replaced by a straight price line with a slope Π_A/Π_B. Since the isoquant curve is also a straight line (with a slope of unity) the minimization of production costs leads to a corner solution. The traveler always chooses the cheapest mode. He prefers mode A to mode B when $\Pi_A < \Pi_B$, otherwise he chooses mode B.

When the trip does not convey any direct utility, the utility derived from a visit is independent of the mode used. The visit's production function [equation (3.3)] can, therefore, be reformulated

$$Z_v = f(X_v, T_v, Z_T), \tag{3.10}$$

FIGURE 2

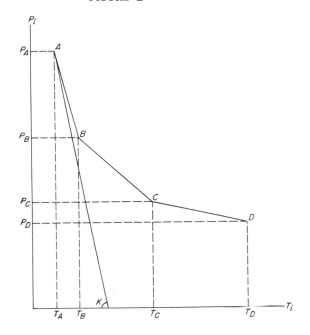

where Z_T denotes the activity, "trip." The distinction between air trip (Z_A) and bus trip (Z_R) can be relaxed and the various modes are regarded merely as different combinations of the time and money inputs required to produce a trip (Z_T). Expanding the model to four modes of transportation, and arranging the various combinations by the increasing order of their time intensity, one can draw the trip's isoquant $ABCD$ (Figure 2), where P_i and T_i denote the money and time inputs required to produce one trip (i.e., one unit of Z_T) by mode i, $i = A$, B, C, D.[1] The slope of any segment of the curve $ABCD$ represents the marginal rate of technical substitition K^* (i.e., the ratio of the

[1] A, B, C, and D may represent four different modes or four different kinds of equipment (e.g., jet and piston planes) that involve a trade-off between time and money. We do not discuss the choice among different kinds of service (e.g., local vs. express, or coach vs. first class), a choice which is primarily affected by availability and the demand for frills, and only very rarely involves a trade-off between time and money.

marginal products of time and money in the production of Z_T). The traveler, aiming at the minimization of costs, chooses mode i if

$$\frac{P_i - P_{i+1}}{T_{i+1} - T_i} = K^*_{i,i+1} < K < K^*_{i-1,i} = \frac{P_{i-1} - P_i}{T_i - T_{i-1}}; \qquad (3.11)$$

where $T_i > T_{i-1}$ and $P_i < P_{i-1}$, $i = A, B, C, D$. In particular, he prefers mode A to B if

$$K > \frac{P_A - P_B}{T_B - T_A} = K^*_{A-B} \qquad \text{(see Figure 2).} \qquad (3.12)$$

Given the time intensities of the various modes, the choice of mode depends solely on the price of time, and given the price of time, the choice is a sole function of the time intensities.[2]

An increase in the price of time increases the price of the trip regardless of mode. The rate of price increase is directly related to the time intensities of the different modes. The relative price of the faster mode (Π_A/Π_B) decreases, and the passenger's tendency to switch to the faster mode increases.[3] The price of time increases with income; hence, one would expect income and the choice of air transportation to be strongly related. Moreover, in the short run, the household may not be able to substitute its free time for work, resulting in a price of time which is higher for business trips than for personal trips. The passenger may, therefore, use air transportation on a business trip but ground transportation on a personal trip of equal length.

The traveler's tendency to switch to air transportation is stronger the smaller the marginal rate of technical substitution K^*, i.e., the smaller the slope of the isoquant in the interval AB. The slope of the isoquant depends on the time intensities of the various modes, and these change with the distance of the trip. Both time and money outlays are

[2] Note that this model does not rule out the possibility that the same individual will use two different modes on two different trips to the same destination, as long as his price of time differs on the two occasions. The passenger may, for example, go by air during the day when his price of time is high, and travel by train at night when his price of time is lower.

[3] The change in relative prices does not assure the passenger's switch to the faster mode as the slower mode may still be (absolutely) cheaper ($\Pi_A > \Pi_B$). Put differently, the increase in the slope of the price line in Figure 2 does not necessarily lead to a shift from B to A, because of the kink at point B.

functions of the distance traveled. The production of a trip involves a fixed cost component of the time and money spent on the way or at the terminal, and a variable cost component related to distance. The relationship between the cost components and the distance (M) can be approximated by a linear function

$$T_i = \alpha_{0i} + \alpha_{1i}M$$
$$P_i = \beta_{0i} + \beta_{1i}M \tag{3.13}$$
$$\Pi_i = (\alpha_{0i}K + \beta_{0i}) + (\alpha_{1i}K + \beta_{1i})M.$$

The goods-intensive mode A is preferred to B when the price of time

$$K > \frac{(\beta_{0A} - \beta_{0B}) + (\beta_{1A} - \beta_{1B})M}{(\alpha_{0B} - \alpha_{0A}) + (\alpha_{1B} - \alpha_{1A})M} = K^*. \tag{3.14}$$

No passenger will use mode A if $T_A > T_B$, i.e., assuming $\alpha_{1B} > \alpha_{1A}$

$$M < \frac{\alpha_{0A} - \alpha_{0B}}{\alpha_{1B} - \alpha_{1A}}, \tag{3.15}$$

and every passenger will prefer the faster mode if $P_B > P_A$, i.e., assuming $\beta_{1A} > \beta_{1B}$

$$M < \frac{\beta_{0B} - \beta_{0A}}{\beta_{1A} - \beta_{1B}}. \tag{3.16}$$

The marginal rate of technical substitution K^* is inversely related to the distance of the trip when an increase in the distance increases the time differential $(T_B - T_A)$ at a faster rate than the increase in the money differential $(P_A - P_B)$

$$\frac{\partial K^*}{\partial M} < 0 = > \frac{\partial(T_B - T_A)/\partial M}{T_B - T_A} > \frac{\partial(P_A - P_B)/\partial M}{P_A - P_B} \tag{3.17}$$

i.e., when

$$\frac{\beta_{0A} - \beta_{0B}}{\beta_{1A} - \beta_{1B}} > \frac{\alpha_{0B} - \alpha_{0A}}{\alpha_{1B} - \alpha_{1A}}. \tag{3.18}$$

In this case the passenger does not use the faster mode unless the distance of the trip

$$M > \frac{(\beta_{0A} - \beta_{0B}) + (\alpha_{0A} - \alpha_{0B})K}{(\beta_{1B} - \beta_{1A}) + (\alpha_{1B} - \alpha_{1A})K} = M^*. \tag{3.19}$$

FIGURE 3

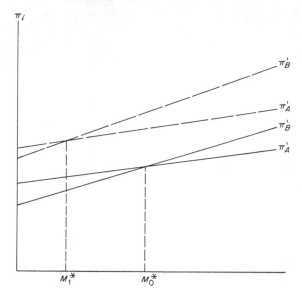

The switching distance M^* (the distance at which the passenger switches from slower to faster modes) is inversely related to the price of time. An increase in the price of time affects mode A less than mode B, and cuts the switching distance from M_0^* to M_1^* (see Figure 3). High income passengers are expected to use airline transportation for shorter distances than low income passengers. The same holds for business vs. personal travelers. Only those travelers whose price of time is

$$K < \frac{\beta_{1A} - \beta_{1B}}{\alpha_{1B} - \alpha_{1A}} \tag{3.20}$$

will never use the faster mode.[4]

An increase in income increases the demand for visits and trips, but increases also the price of time and, hence, the prices of these two activities. An increase in income from Y_0 to Y_1 (Figure 4) shifts the demand for "trips to point i" from D_0 to D_1. However, the accompany-

---

[4] (3.20) and (3.15) are the asymptotes of the rectangular hyperbola (3.14).

ing change in the price of time raises the price of the trip from Π_0 to Π_1, and shifts the income-consumption curve from C_0 to C_1. The net income effect X_0X_2 is the difference between the income effect X_0X_1 and the price effect X_1X_2. The net income effect is directly related to the income elasticity of trips, and inversely related to the trip's price elasticity, the elasticity of the price of time with respect to income $[\eta_{KY} = (dK/dY) \cdot (Y/K)]$, and the time intensity of the mode used. The passenger's tendency to use the faster (less time-intensive) mode increases with his income. Thus, other things being equal, the net income effect and income are positively correlated.

FIGURE 4

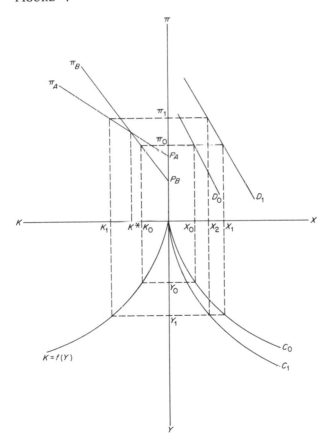

FOUR

THE DOMESTIC TRANSPORTATION MARKET

IN 1963, UNITED STATES households and firms produced 257 million domestic trips. Two out of every three American adults participated in this production process, and the average number of travelers per trip was 1.9. One out of every five domestic trips was produced by firms for business purposes; the rest were produced by households for personal purposes.[1]

The demand for trips is directly related to income. Only one out of every ten adults with an income under $2,000 belongs to the class of frequent travelers (i.e., travelers who take five trips or more annually), while about half of the adults with an income over $15,000 belong to this class. Alternatively, over one-half of all adults with an income under $2,000 did not take any trip during 1962, while only one-sixth of the adults in the $15,000+ class were nontravelers.[2]

---

[1] These figures are based on two transportation surveys conducted in the late fifties and early sixties. The first survey, conducted by the Social Research Center, Ann Arbor, Michigan, is summarized in J. B. Lansing and D. M. Blood's *The Changing Travel Market,* Ann Arbor, Michigan, 1964. The second survey, conducted by the Bureau of the Census, is summed up in *Census of Transportation, 1963,* Vol. I, *Passenger Transportation Survey,* Washington, D.C., 1966. For our purposes we can ignore the slight differences in the populations covered by these two surveys: (a) the Michigan survey covers the adult population in 1962, while the Census survey covers the whole population in 1963; and (b) the Michigan survey defines a trip as any travel to a place at least 100 miles away by one or more members of the household, while the Census survey also includes trips of less than 100 miles if they involve staying out of town overnight or longer. Both surveys exclude commuters.

[2] Lansing and Blood, *op. cit.,* pp. 14–15, 217.

TABLE 1

Distribution of Total Trips and Total Travelers by Means of Transportation and Distance of Trip: 1963

Distance of Trip (miles)	All Transpor- tation	Auto	Bus	Air Carrier	Rail- road	Other
			TRIPS			
Distribution by Means of Transportation						
All trips	100	84	4	5	3	4
U.S. trips						
Under 50	100	90	6	—	1	3
50—99	100	92	3	—	3	2
100—199	100	90	4	2	2	2
200—499	100	72	5	13	4	6
500 or more	100	47	4	33	8	8
Outside U.S.ª	100	59	4	21	1	15
Distribution by Distance of Trip						
All trips	100	100	100	100	100	100
U.S. trips						
Under 50	23	25	29	—	10	21
50—99	23	26	18	—	24	10
100—199	28	30	26	10	22	19
200—499	16	14	18	37	24	25
500 or more	8	4	7	45	19	17
Outside U.S.ª	2	1	2	8	1	8
			TRAVELER			
Distribution by Means of Transportation						
All trips	100	89	3	4	2	2
U.S. trips						
Under 50	100	94	3	—	1	2
50—99	100	95	2	—	2	1
100—199	100	93	2	1	2	2
200—499	100	82	3	8	3	4
500 or more	100	61	3	23	7	6
Outside U.S.ª	100	67	2	16	1	14
Distribution by Distance of Trip						
All trips	100	100	100	100	100	100
U.S. trips						
Under 50	21	22	27	1	8	19
50—99	25	26	19	—	21	9
100—199	29	30	26	9	23	18
200—499	16	15	18	35	25	25
500 or more	7	5	8	46	22	18
Outside U.S.ª	2	2	2	9	1	11

SOURCE: *Census of Transportation, 1963*, Vol. I, *Passenger Transportation Survey*, p. 18.
ªIncludes destinations in Canada, Mexico, and U.S. outlying areas.

The number of trips is inversely related to distance. Almost one half of all trips are overnight trips to a distance of under 100 miles, but only 8 per cent of the trips range beyond 500 miles (see Table 1). This relationship can be interpreted as a negative price effect, provided there is not a negative correlation between the attractiveness of the point of destination and the trip's distance.

The bulk of all trips was produced by private cars. Six out of every seven trips and nine out of every ten traveler-trips used this mode. Consequently, the share of public transportation and the share of the individual common carriers in the transportation market were quite small. The air carriers, the most popular among the common carriers, did not account for more than 5 per cent of the trips and 4 per cent of the traveler-trips. The respective shares of the bus and the railroads were 4 and 3 per cent of the trips, and 3 and 2 per cent of the traveler-trips. Only one out of every nine adults traveled by air, about one out of every twelve traveled by bus, and one out of every fourteen traveled by train.

What are the factors determining the modal split? The passenger's choice of mode depends on his price of time, and the time and money outlays involved in traveling by the various modes. There is no information on the passenger's price of time, and the data on the time and money inputs suffer from gross inaccuracies. The elapsed time of a trip depends not only on the mode used, but also on the distance to and from the terminals (i.e., airports, railroad stations, and bus terminals), the specific schedule, the number and length of stops en route, weather conditions, road congestion, etc. Similarly, the money outlays depend on a multiplicity of factors: class of service (e.g., first class vs. coach), additional en route expenditures (e.g., food, lodging), etc. In the absence of detailed data, one can use some rough approximations—the elapsed time of the fastest scheduled trip and the money outlays on coach service.[3] These data, though crude, provide sufficient

---

[3] The data relating to air trips are based on *The Quick Reference Official Airline Guide,* 1963. The rail and bus data were extracted from *The Official Guide of the Railways,* 1963, and from *Russel's Official National Motorcoach Guide,* 1963, respectively. Data on rail and bus fares were obtained directly from the New York Central and the Pennsylvania Railroad companies and from the Greyhound and Trailways bus companies. Auto traveling data are based on American Automobile Association estimates. Both rail and bus data do not include the time and money inputs involved in reaching and leaving the terminals.

information for the interpretation of the more obvious patterns of the modal split.

As indicated in the last chapter, both time and money outlays are linear functions of the distance traveled. Relating the data for these outlays for 38 routes originating in New York to their corresponding distances we found

$$T_A = 2.56 + .00210 \, M + U$$
$$(0.08) \quad (.00008)$$
$$r^2 = .95$$

$$T_R = -0.59 + .02542 \, M + U$$
$$(0.54) \quad (.00050)$$
$$r^2 = .99$$

$$T_B = -0.32 + .02841 \, M + U$$
$$(0.58) \quad (.00054)$$
$$r^2 = .99$$

$$T_C = 0.89 + .02817 \, M + U$$
$$(.00041)$$
$$r^2 = .99 \qquad (4.1)$$

$$P_A = 7.04 + .06006 \, M + U$$
$$(.75) \quad (.0007)$$
$$r^2 = .99$$

$$P_R = 5.59 + .04265 \, M + U$$
$$(1.52) \quad (.0014)$$
$$r^2 = .96$$

$$P_B = 3.56 + .03264 \, M + U$$
$$(.51) \quad (.0005)$$
$$r^2 = .99$$

$$P_C = \qquad .072 \quad M,$$

where A, R, B, and C denote air, rail, bus, and private car, respectively, P_i is the fare (in dollars), T_i is the elapsed time (in hours), and M is the shortest air distance (in miles). Air transportation is by far the fastest of all modes. The plane's effective speed of 480 miles per hour is more than ten times as fast as any ground transportation, the train's effective speed being 40 mph and the motor vehicle's effective speed being 35 mph.[4] A thousand mile trip that lasts less than 5 hours by

[4] The effective speed is not merely a function of cruising speed, but also of the number and length of stops, and the degree of circuity.

plane lasts close to 25 hours by rail and over 28 hours by the automotive modes.

The opposite hierarchy is observed when we consider public transportation's pecuniary costs. The plane, the fastest among the modes, is the most expensive, while the bus, the slowest, is the cheapest. However, the differences between the pecuniary costs of the public modes of transportation are much smaller than the differences in elapsed time. A one thousand mile trip costs $36 by bus, $48 by train, and no more than $67 by plane.

TABLE 2

Distribution of Total Trips and Total Travelers by Means of Transportation and by Family Income: 1963

(per cent)

Annual Family Income (dollars)	All Transportation	Auto	Bus	Air Carrier	Rail-road	Other
			TRIPS			
Distribution by Means of Transportation						
All income	100	84	4	5	3	4
Under 1,000	100	83	8	1	2	6
1,000—1,999	100	81	7	2	3	7
2,000—2,999	100	83	9	2	3	3
3,000—3,999	100	85	6	2	4	3
4,000—4,999	100	86	5	3	3	3
5,000—5,999	100	90	3	3	2	2
6,000—7,499	100	87	3	3	4	3
7,500—9,999	100	88	2	4	2	4
10,000—14,999	100	78	2	13	3	4
15,000 and over	100	74	2	17	2	5
Income not reported	100	79	6	8	5	2
Distribution by Family Income						
All income	100	100	100	100	100	100
Under 1,000	6	6	12	1	4	9
1,000—1,999	5	5	9	2	5	10
2,000—2,999	5	5	12	1	6	4
3,000—3,999	7	6	10	2	9	6
4,000—4,999	10	10	12	5	11	7
5,000—5,999	10	11	6	5	8	7
6,000—7,499	14	14	11	7	19	11
7,500—9,999	16	17	8	12	10	15
10,000—14,999	12	12	7	30	10	15
15,000 and over	8	7	3	24	6	11
Income not reported	7	7	10	11	12	5

(*continued*)

TABLE 2 (Cont.)

Annual Family Income (dollars)	All Transportation	Auto	Bus	Air Carrier	Railroad	Other
			TRAVELER			
Distribution by Means of Transportation						
All income	100	89	3	4	2	2
Under 1,000	100	85	8	1	1	5
1,000—1,999	100	85	6	2	2	5
2,000—2,999	100	89	6	1	2	2
3,000—3,999	100	91	4	1	2	2
4,000—4,999	100	91	4	2	2	1
5,000—5,999	100	93	2	2	2	1
6,000—7,499	100	92	2	2	2	2
7,500—9,999	100	93	1	3	1	2
10,000—14,999	100	85	2	8	2	3
15,000 and over	100	80	1	13	2	4
Income not reported	100	86	3	5	4	2
Distribution by Family Income						
All income	100	100	100	100	100	100
Under 1,000	4	3	11	1	3	8
1,000—1,999	4	4	9	2	5	8
2,000—2,999	5	5	11	1	5	5
3,000—3,999	7	7	10	3	8	5
4,000—4,999	10	10	13	5	11	6
5,000—5,999	11	12	7	5	10	7
6,000—7,499	15	16	11	8	18	11
7,500—9,999	17	18	8	12	10	16
10,000—14,999	13	12	8	28	11	17
15,000 and over	7	6	3	25	7	12
Income not reported	7	7	9	10	12	5

SOURCE: The advance report of the *1963 Census of Transportation, Passenger Transportation Survey—National Travel, 1963 Summary.*

This reverse order of ranking for the three common carriers when ranked by time and by money outlays rules out the possibility of a uniform choice for all travelers. For most of the trips ranging beyond 135 miles there is a trade-off between time and money. The crucial factor determining the passenger's choice is his price of time, which is a monotonically increasing function of income. The passenger's tendency to use the fastest mode, the plane, is expected to increase with his income. Thus, while travelers with an income under $4,000 use this mode for less than one-fiftieth of their trips, a traveler with an income of $15,000 or more is likely to use it in more than one-sixth of all cases (see Table 2). Conversely, while over 7 per cent of the trips of the low income group were conducted by bus, this mode was used for only 2 per cent of the trips by the high income group.

A similar pattern is observed when we examine the effect of the purpose of the trip on the modal split. Traveling time can be more easily transformed into work when the trip is for business purposes than when it is for personal purposes. The foregone earning and the opportunity cost of time may, therefore, be higher in the first instance, and so may be the passenger's inclination to use the faster mode. These expectations are borne out by Table 3. Air transportation is used on no more than 3 per cent of all personal trips, as compared with 17 per cent of the business trips. On the other hand, only 2 per cent of business trips are conducted by bus, as compared with 5 per cent of the personal trips.[5]

The unique hierarchy of time and pecuniary costs is blurred, somewhat, if private modes of transportation are included in the analysis. The tacit assumption that the production function of trips is linear homogeneous in the time and money inputs serves as a close approximation in the case of public modes of transportation. In this case, the marginal costs of a trip are constant, and do not vary with the number of travelers participating in the trip. The assumption of constant returns to scale is not satisfied when a private mode of transportation is used in the production process. The pecuniary costs of a private mode are insensitive to the size of the party participating in the trip, as long as the party size does not exceed the capacity of the vehicle used (say, $n \leq 5$ in the case of a private car). The average cost per passenger is a decreasing function of the party size. A group of n passengers, who assign a high value to traveling en bloc, prefers a public mode of transportation (say, air transportation) to traveling by car only if the costs of the trip by car, for the group as a whole, exceed the trip's cost by air,

$$\sum_{i=1}^{n} \Pi_{iA} < \sum_{i=1}^{n} \Pi_{iC} \Leftrightarrow \bar{K} > \frac{P_A - (P_c/n)}{T_C - T_A}, \tag{4.2}$$

where $\bar{K} = \sum_{i=1}^{n} K_i/n$ is the group's average price of time. Given the average

[5] The interpretation of Tables 2 and 3 is somewhat oversimplified since it tends to overlook existing spurious correlations. Passenger's income and the trip's purpose and distance do not act independently. The two-way classification of the Bureau of the Census' published data does not allow the separation of the effects of these three variables.

price of time of the group, the tendency to travel by a public mode decreases with party size. Thus, as Table 4 indicates, over one half of the auto trips involved at least a party of two, while only one out of every six trips by public transportation involved a party of a similar size. Put differ-

TABLE 3

Distribution of Total Trips and Total Travelers by Means of Transportation and by Purpose of Trip: 1963

Purpose of Trip	All Transportation	Auto	Bus	Air Carrier	Railroad	Other
			TRIPS			
Distribution by Means of Transportation						
All purposes	100	84	4	5	3	4
Business	100	74	2	17	2	5
Visits to friends and relatives	100	86	5	2	4	3
Other pleasure	100	90	3	3	1	3
Personal or family affairs	100	83	6	3	3	5
Distribution by Purpose						
All purposes	100	100	100	100	100	100
Business	21	19	9	64	18	30
Visits to friends and relatives	40	41	50	16	50	31
Other pleasure	21	23	16	11	11	17
Personal or family affairs	18	17	25	9	21	22
			TRAVELER			
Distribution by Means of Transportation						
All purposes	100	89	3	4	2	2
Business	100	77	1	15	2	5
Visits to friends and relatives	100	91	3	2	2	2
Other pleasure	100	93	2	2	1	2
Personal or family affairs	100	88	4	2	3	3
Distribution by Purpose						
All purposes	100	100	100	100	100	100
Business	14	12	8	56	15	26
Visits to friends and relatives	45	46	50	19	51	32
Other pleasure	25	26	18	15	12	21
Personal or family affairs	16	16	24	10	22	21

SOURCE: *Passenger Transportation Survey*, p. 16.

TABLE 4

Distribution of Total Trips and Total Travelers by Means of Transportation and by Size of Party: 1963

(per cent)

Size of Party	All Transportation	Auto	Bus	Air Carrier	Railroad	Other
			TRIPS			
Distribution by Means of Transportation						
All parties	100	84	4	5	3	4
Parties of						
1 person	100	75	7	9	4	5
2 persons	100	91	2	3	2	2
3 or 4 persons	100	96	1	1	1	1
5 or more persons	100	98	—	1	—	1
Distribution by Size of Party						
All parties	100	100	100	100	100	100
Parties of						
1 person	55	49	86	85	77	81
2 persons	23	25	10	11	15	13
3 or 4 persons	16	19	4	3	7	5
5 or more persons	6	7	—	1	1	1
			TRAVELER			
Distribution by Means of Transportation						
All parties	100	89	3	4	2	2
Parties of						
1 person	100	75	7	9	4	5
2 persons	100	91	2	3	2	2
3 or 4 persons	100	96	1	1	1	1
5 or more persons	100	98	—	1	—	1
Distribution by Size of Party						
All parties	100	100	100	100	100	100
Parties of						
1 person	29	24	72	70	58	62
2 persons	24	25	16	18	22	21
3 or 4 persons	30	32	10	8	17	13
5 or more persons	17	19	2	4	3	4

SOURCE: *Passenger Transportation Survey*, p. 24.

ently, while less than one-quarter of all car travelers traveled without accompaniment, over two-thirds of the travelers by public transportation went singly. Given the party size (n), the time and money outlays (P_A, P_C, T_A, and T_C), the tendency to travel by car is inversely related to the average price of time. In particular, when the group consists of m adults whose price of time is K, and ($n - m$) children whose price of time is zero, then $\bar{K} = \dfrac{m}{n} K$, and the travelers' inclination to use a car is directly related to the percentage of children in the group.[6]

An additional factor enhancing the comparative advantage of the car is its effect on other inputs used in the production of the visit. The private car satisfies the traveler's need for mobility at the point of destination. A traveler by public modes of transportation may obtain the same mobility but only at additional costs (e.g., the costs of intracity public transportation, taxi, or rented car). Let R denote these additional costs, then the public mode is used only if

$$\bar{K} > \frac{P_A - (P_C - R)/n}{T_C - T_A}. \tag{4.3}$$

The comparative advantage of the car is directly related to R. Direct evidence of this relationship is provided by the Michigan survey and by other surveys.[7] Some indirect evidence is contained in Table 3. The need for an auxiliary means of transportation varies with the purpose of the trip, being of special importance in the case of pleasure trips (e.g., sight-seeing and other forms of outdoor recreation). We would expect, therefore, as Table 3 duly testifies, that the percentage of auto trips for pleasure purposes (recorded in the table as "other pleasure") exceeds the share of auto trips for any other purpose of trip. Ninety per cent of all pleasure trips were conducted by car compared with 82 per cent for all other purposes of trip.[8]

---

[6] These conclusions are supported by the Michigan survey findings, Lansing and Blood, *op. cit.*, pp. 44, 70, 71.

[7] *Ibid.*, p. 44, and Opinion Research Corporation, *The Domestic Travel Market*, Vol. I, Princeton, N.J., 1962.

[8] A further factor affecting the choice of car is the accounting method used by the driver. According to the American Automobile Association's "Your Driving Costs," the marginal pecuniary costs in 1963 (gas and oil, tires and maintenance) were 3.7¢ per mile. The average costs for a car that covers 10,000 miles annually were 11.6¢ per mile. We used an estimate of 7.2¢ per mile, which was according

The time and money differential varies with the distance of the trip and so does the comparative advantage of the various modes. A passenger who travels in a group of size n (m of whom are adults whose price of time is K) prefers air transportation to traveling by car if his price of time

$$K > \frac{n}{m} \frac{7.04 + [.06006 - (.072/n)]M}{-1.68 + .02606M} = K^*_{A-C},\qquad (4.4)$$

where K and K^* are expressed in terms of dollars per hour, and R is assumed to equal zero. He prefers air to rail if

$$K > \frac{1.45 + .01741M}{-3.15 + .02331M} = K^*_{A-R},\qquad (4.5)$$

and he prefers air to bus if

$$K > \frac{3.48 + .02742M}{-2.88 + .02631M} = K^*_{A-B}.\qquad (4.6)$$

An increase in distance increases the time differential more than the money differential, resulting in a decline of K^*.[9] The passenger's tendency to use the faster mode increases with distance. Put differently, the switching distance from ground to air transportation (M^*) is inversely related to the passenger's price of time.

The three equations describing the relationship between K^* and M are plotted in Charts 1, 2, and 3. Chart 1 traces the factors affecting the choice between air transportation and private car [equation (4.4), given different values of n and m]. The marginal pecuniary costs of a passenger who travels by car without accompaniment ($n = 1$) exceed those of an air traveler. An increase in distance increases the time differential and cuts the money differential between air and car, resulting in an accelerated dissipation of the car's comparative advantage. For any distance beyond

to the Opinion Research survey, *op. cit.*, the average cost the drivers thought they were paying. This estimate is very close to the average compensation paid by firms (8¢ per mile).

[9] Let $T_i = \alpha_{0i} + \alpha_{1i}M$,

$P_i = \beta_{0i} + \beta_{1i}M$,

then

$$\frac{\partial K^*_{i-j}}{\partial M} < 0 \Leftrightarrow (\alpha_{0j} - \alpha_{0i})(\beta_{1i} - \beta_{1j}) < (\alpha_{1j} - \alpha_{1i})(\beta_{0i} - \beta_{0j}).$$

This condition is satisfied in all three cases (4.4), (4.5), and (4.6).

CHART 1

Factors Affecting the Choice Between Air and Private Car Transportation

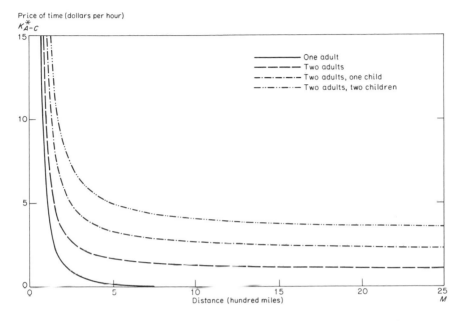

Price of time (dollars per hour)

K^*_{A-C}

Distance (hundred miles)

One adult
Two adults
Two adults, one child
Two adults, two children

590 miles the pecuniary costs to a single traveler by car exceed those by plane, and air transportation becomes both faster and cheaper. When the party size exceeds one, the money differential between air and car increases with distance, though at a slower rate than the increase in the time differential. K^* drops very sharply in the interval $0 < M < 200$, the decline becomes more gradual for the range of 200 to 600 miles, and K^* becomes almost insensitive to changes of distance beyond 600 miles. A similar pattern is observed in Charts 2 and 3, which describe the factors influencing the choice between air and rail and between air and bus, respectively. Thus, relatively small increases in income and in the price of time are sufficient to secure the long range travel market for the airlines, but relatively large increases are required to loosen the ground transportation's hold on the short range market.

Table 1 describes the effect of distance on the modal split. Private cars are used on nine out of ten trips to a distance less than 200 miles, but on less than one half of the trips beyond 500 miles. Air trips, on the other hand, constitute less than one out of every one hundred short

CHART 2

Factors Affecting the Choice Between Air and Rail Transportation

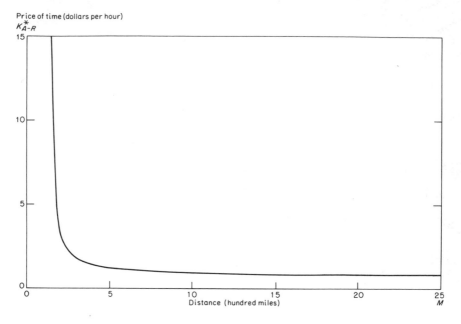

range trips, as compared with one-third of the long range trips. The Michigan survey provides a more detailed breakdown of the trips according to distance and party size. These data show that nonbusiness travelers prefer auto to air in more than seven out of ten trips when the distance exceeds 500 miles. Auto is preferred to air in nine out of ten trips when the party consists of two or more travelers, but it is chosen in only three out of ten cases when the traveler has to go alone.[10]

The switching distance (M^*) decreases with the price of time, resulting in an observed inverse relationship between the passenger's income and the range of his air trip.[11] Only 21 per cent of the air travelers going less than 250 miles have an income of less than $10,000. This income group comprises 31 per cent of the air travelers when the

[10] Lansing and Blood, *op. cit.,* p. 55 and Table 43, p. 248.

[11] The Port of New York Authority, *New York's Domestic Air Passenger Market, April 1963 through March 1964,* New York, May 1965, p. 15.

CHART 3

Factors Affecting the Choice Between Air and Bus Transportation

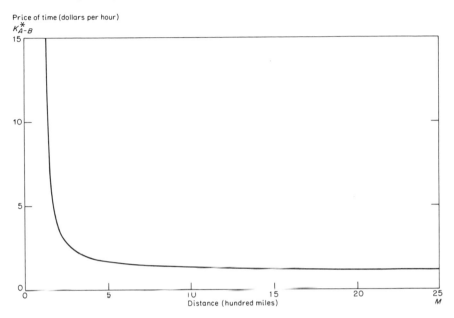

Price of time (dollars per hour)

K^*_{A-B}

Distance (hundred miles)

M

distance exceeds 800 miles. Business travelers assign a higher value to their time than personal travelers with the same income, and tend, therefore, to enter the air travel market sooner. The incidence of personal travelers increases with the length of the haul. The share of non-business air travelers is less than one half of the share of business air travelers when the distance is less than 800 miles, but the two shares are equal beyond that distance.[12]

A passenger prefers rail to bus if

$$K > \frac{2.03 + .01001M}{.27 + .00300M} = K^*_{R-B}. \qquad (4.7)$$

Combining equations (4.5), (4.6), and (4.7), we obtain a further insight into the factors affecting the choice of public mode of transportation. Chart 4 shows the effect of distance and the price of time on

[12] *Ibid.*

CHART 4

Factors Affecting the Choice Between Air, Rail, and Bus Transportation

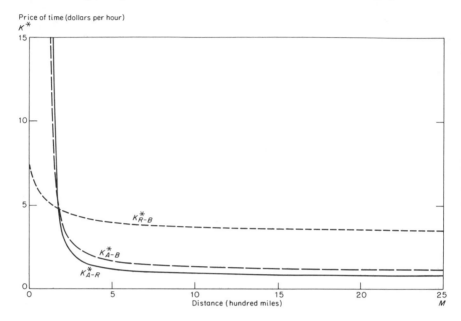

the three-way choice of air, rail, or bus. For example, a passenger prefers to use air rather than rail transportation for a trip of 150 miles only if his price of time exceeds $11.80 per hour, he prefers air to bus if his price of time exceeds $7.10 per hour, and he prefers rail to bus if his price of time exceeds $5.30 per hour. Bus transportation is, therefore, used for 150 mile trips only by individuals whose price of time is less than $5.30 per hour, rail transportation by individuals whose price of time is between $5.30 and $11.80 per hour, and air transportation by individuals whose price of time exceeds $11.80 per hour. Air transportation does not offer any time saving relative to rail as long as the distance of the trip is less than 135 miles. The public transportation travel market for a trip of less than 135 miles is, therefore, divided between the bus, which serves the low income passengers, and the railroad, which serves the high income passengers. Air carriers become an effective competitor only for a trip beyond 135 miles, cutting sharply into the railroad's share of the market. The railroad is squeezed out of the market when the distance of the trip exceeds 176 miles. When the distance is 176 miles a passenger prefers rail over the bus only if his price of time exceeds $4.70 per hour. However, if his price of time exceeds $4.70 per hour he prefers air to rail, resulting in the elimination of rail from the competition. The travel market for a distance beyond 176 miles is divided between the bus and the airline industry. Only a passenger whose price of time is less than $1.00 per hour will always use bus. The recent decision by some railroad companies to stop all passenger services for a distance beyond 200 miles,[13] as well as the great secular decline of the railroads' share in the passenger transportation market, is consistent with the prediction of this simple model.

Finally, Tables 1 and 2 and Charts 1 and 3 provide a crude measure of the relationship between the price of time and hourly earnings. Table 1 indicates that about 70 per cent of all common-carrier travelers to a distance exceeding 500 miles use air transportation. Given the income distribution of these travelers (Table 5), and assuming that the choice of mode is made solely on the basis of income, the minimum family income of air travelers is $4,700. The corresponding hourly earnings are $2.20 per hour. The income figures are based on the interpolation of data presented in Table 5.[14] Figure 7 suggests that the minimum price of time of air travelers going more than 500 miles is between $1.10 and $1.70 per hour. Assuming an average value of $K^* = \$1.40$ per hour, the price of time is found to be about 60 per cent of the traveler's hourly earnings.

A similar relationship is observed if one examines the modal split between auto and air travelers for the distance between 200 and 500 miles. The private car dominates this range, constituting 91 per cent of the combined traveler-trips of auto and air. Following our previous assumption, the minimum income of air travelers for this distance is $14,400 and their minimum hourly earnings are $3.90. Assuming that the average party size of auto travelers equals two (two being the average party size of auto travelers for all distances), the minimum price of time of air travelers is about $2.30 per hour, i.e., about 60 per cent of their hourly earnings.

---

[13] *New York Times,* July 27, 1966.

[14] The relationship between family income and hourly earnings is described in the next chapter.

TABLE 5

Distribution of Total Travelers by Means of Transportation and by Family Income: 1963

(per cent)

Annual Family Income (dollars)	Common Carrier Travelers		Auto and Air Travelers	
	Percentage	Cumulative Percentage	Percentage	Cumulative Percentage
All Income	100.0		100.0	
Under 1,000	5.3	5.3	3.1	3.1
1,000—1,999	5.6	10.9	4.2	7.3
2,000—2,999	5.8	16.7	5.2	12.5
3,000—3,999	7.2	23.9	7.4	19.9
4,000—4,999	10.0	33.9	10.5	30.4
5,000—5,999	7.5	41.4	12.6	43.0
6,000—7,499	12.5	53.9	16.9	59.9
7,500—9,999	11.4	65.3	19.1	79.0
10,000—14,999	19.5	84.8	13.7	92.7
15,000 and over	15.2	100.0	7.3	100.0

SOURCE: Table 2.

A somewhat higher estimate of the ratio of the price of time to hourly earnings is reached when one analyzes the auto-air split of travelers going more than 500 miles. At this range the share of auto travelers falls to 73 per cent, implying that the air traveler's minimum income and minimum hourly earnings are $9,200 and $3.00 per hour, respectively. According to the Michigan survey, the average number of auto travelers in a party for this range is three. Assuming that this party consists of two adults and a child, the minimum price of time of air travelers is, according to Chart 1, about $2.70 per hour, i.e., about 90 per cent of their hourly earnings.[15]

[15] The computation of the average party size is based on Lansing and Blood, *op. cit.*, Table 43, p. 248. Had we assumed the same party size for auto trips of 200 to 500 miles, the estimate of the minimum price of time of air travelers and the ratio of this price to hourly earnings would have to be raised to $4.40 and $1.10 per hour, respectively.

The last estimate agrees very well with an estimate based on the distribution of travelers using public modes of transportation for a distance of between 200 and 500 miles. Air carriers capture 57 per cent of this market, suggesting that the minimum income of air travelers is $6,200 and minimum hourly earnings are $2.60. The minimum price of time of these travelers is about $2.40 per hour (see Chart 3), i.e., about 90 per cent of their hourly earnings.

FIVE

The Estimation of the Price of Time and the Demand for Airline Transportation

AS DEMONSTRATED in the last chapter, crude data can go a long way in interpreting the broader outlines of the transportation market. Timetables and fare schedules provide enough information to explain the effect of income, of the purpose of a trip, and of distance on the modal choice, and to yield a rough estimate of the relationship between the price of time and hourly earnings. The prediction of the future shape of the transportation market calls, however, for a more sophisticated approach based on the estimation of the traveler's demand and his price of time.

Assume that the quantity of trips to destination j demanded by traveler $i(X_{ij})$ is an exponential function of the trip's price (Π_{ij}) and the traveler's income (Y_i),

$$X_{ij} = B_j \Pi_{ij}{}^{\beta_{1j}} Y_i{}^{\beta_{2j}} e^{u_{ij}}, \tag{5.1}$$

where u_{ij} denotes the stochastic disturbance term. As explained in Chapter 3 the income variable Y_i serves either as a measure of the traveler's ability to pay for the trip or as a proxy for his skills. The price of the trip Π_{ij} varies both with the destination of the trip and with the traveler's price of time. Rewriting the demand function in a logarithmic form (natural log) yields a linear function,

$$\log X_{ij} = \beta_{0j} + \beta_{1j} \log \Pi_{ij} + \beta_{2j} \log Y_i + u_{ij}, \tag{5.2}$$

where $\beta_{0j} = \log B_j$. Unfortunately, this function's parameters cannot be estimated directly since one of the independent variables, price, is unobservable; the price of time being unknown,

$$\log X_{ij} = \beta_{0j} + \beta_{1j} \log (P_j + K_i T_j) + \beta_{2j} \log Y_i + u_{ij}.^{[1]} \quad (5.3)$$

Economic theory suggests that the price of time and earnings are directly related. It does not specify, however, the exact nature of this relationship. The value the traveler places on his time may change at a faster rate than his hourly earnings, it may increase with the time of traveling, and may depend on the mode used. Adopting the simplest set of assumptions, I assumed that the price of time is proportional to hourly earnings (W) and is independent of the elapsed time and the mode of travel,

$$K_i = kW_i, \quad (5.4)$$

Equation (5.3) can, therefore, be written

$$\log X_{ij} = \beta_{0j} + \beta_{1j} \log (P_j + kW_i T_j) + \beta_{2j} \log Y_i + u_{ij}. \quad (5.5)$$

The demand functions for trips to various destinations differ with the "attractiveness" of the point of destination, the "attractiveness" being determined by factors affecting the demand for visits, the degree of substitution between trips and related inputs, the price of these inputs, and the share of the trip's price in the total costs of the visit. Assuming that these factors affect only the level of the demand curves but not the demand elasticities, (5.5) can be rewritten

$$X_{ij} = \beta_{0j} + \beta_1 \log (P_j + kW_i T_j) + \beta_2 \log Y_i + u_{ij}. \quad (5.6)$$

When the attractiveness factor (G_j) is measurable and additive, one can rewrite equation (5.6),

$$X_{ij} = \beta_0 + \beta_1 \log (P_j + kW_i T_j) + \beta_2 \log Y_i + \beta_3 \log G_j + u_{ij}. \quad (5.7)$$

[1]Note the difference between this formulation and a model that specifies that the fare (P) and time (T) elasticities are constant

$$\log X_{ij} = \beta_{0j} + \beta_{1j} \log P_j + \beta_{2j} \log T_j + \beta_{3j} \log Y_i + u_{ij}.$$

(See, for example, Samuel L. Brown, "Measuring the Elasticities of Air Travel," 125th Annual Meeting of the American Statistical Association, September 1965.) Equation (5.3) is nonlinear in $\log P$ and $\log T$.

Substituting in equation (5.6) arbitrarily chosen values of k and picking the value that yields the highest explanatory power, one can obtain the estimate of both the price and income elasticities (β_1 and β_2, respectively), as well as the ratio of the price of time to hourly earnings (k).[2]

Information on the population's traveling habits can be obtained in two ways: (a) a ticket count, and (b) a survey based on personal interviews. The major drawback of the first method is its inability to provide any additional information on the traveler's and the trip's characteristics other than the trip's destination. In particular, this method does not disclose any information on the traveler's income and the purpose of the trip. An attempt to incorporate these two variables in the demand analysis calls, therefore, for the use of some auxiliary data, data that are necessarily inaccurate or unavailable. In order to avoid these problems, it was decided to base the analysis on interview data.

One of the more detailed sources of interview data is contained in the Port of New York Authority's survey.[3] The survey covered a representative sample of all outbound flights of scheduled airlines departing from the three New York airports during the twelve months ending March 29, 1964. The cluster sample included 1,358 randomly chosen flights. Information concerning 22,263 passengers on' these flights was processed, representing 0.27 per cent of all outbound passengers from New York in the same period. Each of these passengers (twelve years of age or older) was asked to fill out a questionnaire regarding his socioeconomic characteristics (i.e., age, sex, education, profession, industry, family income, and place of residence), his flight experience (i.e., the number of air trips in the last twelve months, and the date of his first airline flight), and the present trip's characteristics (i.e., origin and destination, purpose, duration, the class of the ticket, and the mode of arrival at the airport). The survey provides no information on the

[2] Had we assumed that the demand function is linear

$$X_{ij} = \beta_0 + \beta_1 \Pi_{ij} + \beta_2 Y_i + \beta_3 G_j + u_{ij},$$

we could estimate

$$\begin{aligned} X_{ij} &= \beta_0 + \beta_1(P_j + kW_iT_j) + \beta_2 Y_i + \beta_3 G_j + u_{ij} \\ &= \beta_0 + \beta_1 P_j + \beta_1 kW_iT_j + \beta_2 Y_i + \beta_3 G_j + u_{ij} \\ &= \beta_0 + \beta_1 P_j + \gamma W_iT_j + \beta_2 Y_i + \beta_3 G_j + u_{ij}, \end{aligned}$$

where $k = \gamma/\beta_1$.

[3] *New York's Domestic Air Passenger Market, April 1963 through March 1964,* New York, May 1965.

characteristics of the different trips taken by a given traveler, but rather a detailed description of the properties of each air passenger-trip.

The dependent variable in our model describes the number of trips to a given destination taken by an individual (or a household) with a given income. The first step in adapting the Port of New York Authority data to our model calls, therefore, for the classification of the information on passenger-trips by the traveler's income and destination. In order to reduce the amount of random "noise," we focused our attention on the 38 most heavily trafficked routes originating in New York, comprising a subsample of 13,822 nontransfer passenger-trips. The Port of New York Authority questionnaire distinguished among ten income groups. The classification by income and destination, therefore, results in 380 observations, each describing the total number of air trips to a certain destination taken by travelers belonging to a given income group. To obtain a measure of the trips per family, one has to divide these figures by the number of potential travelers. Assuming that all travelers to a certain destination reside either in New York's or in the destination's Standard Metropolitan Statistical Areas (transfer passengers being excluded from the subsample), the number of passenger-trips in each cell was divided by the number of families belonging to that income class in the two SMSAs.[4] This procedure was followed separately for business and nonbusiness trips to produce two dependent variables—the number of business trips per family and the number of personal trips per family.

A second variable based on the Port of New York Authority data is the income variable. The questionnaire distinguished among 10 income groups: 0–3,000; 3,000–5,000; 5,000–6,000; 6,000–7,000; 7,000–10,000; 10,000–11,000; 11,000–15,000; 15,000–20,000; 20,000–25,000; and 25,000+ dollars. The groups' midpoints were chosen as the representative incomes of those passengers whose income did not exceed $10,000; the mean values of a fitted Pareto distribution were used for the higher income groups.

The corresponding data on hourly earnings are based on the 1/1,000 sample of the 1960 Census of Population. The sample includes information on annual income and earnings in 1959, number of weeks worked during that year, and number of hours worked during the survey week in 1960. To obtain a measure of annual hours we multiplied the number of weekly hours by the number of employment weeks for each person employed both in 1959 and in the survey week (persons employed in agriculture were excluded). Hourly earnings were estimated by dividing a person's annual earning by the estimate of his annual hours of work. This figure was averaged over all the persons in the same income group to yield an estimate of the average hourly earnings.[5] Biases introduced in this measure due to an inaccurate measure of annual working hours have only a slight effect on the estimate of hourly earnings for the upper income groups, who constitute the major part of air travelers.

Seventy-eight per cent of all business travelers in the sample belong to the professional, technical, official, or managerial occupations. Therefore, as a measure of a business traveler's hourly earnings we used the value of the average earnings of these occupations. Moreover, ninety-one per cent of all business air travelers in the sample are males. Hence, we used as an alternative measure the hourly earnings figures of males belonging to those occupations.

Similarly, we employed two measures for the hourly earnings of personal travelers. As the first measure we used average hourly earnings for all the employed persons in 1959. However, because of the difference in the sex composition in the data for employed persons and that for personal travelers we computed a second measure—a weighted average of male or female hourly earnings, using the percentage of males and females among personal travelers (45 and 55 per cent, respectively) as weights.[6]

[5] For a description of the 1/1,000 sample and an evaluation of the reliability of the hours data, see Victor R. Fuchs, *Differentials in Hourly Earnings by Region and City Size, 1959,* Occasional Paper 101, National Bureau of Economic Research, New York, 1967. Note, however, that our measure of hourly earnings differs from the aggregate measure used by Fuchs.

[6] The estimates of hourly earnings for all employed, for males, for females, for all professional occupations, and for males in professional occupations are contained in Table 6.

TABLE 6

Average Hourly Earnings Classified by Income Groups

(dollars per hour)

Annual Family Income (dollars)	All Employed	Male	Female	Professionals and Managers	
				All	Male
Under 3,000	1.62	1.71	1.52	1.46	1.48
3,000—4,999	2.07	2.15	1.90	2.44	1.99
5,000—5,999	2.43	2.53	2.16	2.59	2.50
6,000—6,999	2.60	2.77	2.16	2.83	2.69
7,000—9,999	2.85	3.12	2.27	3.28	3.35
10,000—14,999	3.39	3.82	2.58	4.13	4.41
15,000—24,999	4.87	5.65	2.97	6.17	6.73
25,000 and over	12.96	14.30	6.99	14.05	14.95
All employed	2.75	3.06	2.12	3.77	4.10

We were not able to secure information on the identity of the flights included in the sample. Thus we had to substitute some average figures based on the *Official Air Line Guide* for 1963, for the exact measures of the fare and the elapsed time of the trips. The elapsed time depends on the type of equipment used for the flight (i.e., piston, turboprop, or turbojet), and on the time needed to reach the airport. The money outlays are a function of equipment used (jet vs. nonjet), class of service (first class vs. coach), and expenditures on the way to the terminal. We computed two weighted averages of the fastest time and the most prevalent time of the different kinds of equipment, weighted by the share of each equipment in the daily schedule, but found that these measures are almost perfectly correlated with a simpler measure—the fastest scheduled flight on each route. Likewise, we computed a weighted average of first class and economy fares corrected for jet surcharges, to find that this variable is almost perfectly correlated with the economy (coach) fares (almost two-thirds of the passengers in the sample used this class of service). For the sake of simplicity we used, therefore, the estimate of the coach fare and fastest elapsed time, to which we added the Guide's estimates of the limousine fare and the average driving time from city center to the airport at both terminals.

The last variable required for the estimation of equation (5.7) is a measure of the "attractiveness" of the point of destination. This variable is a function of population size, level of economic activity, scenery, points of interest, etc. A common procedure calls for the quantification of these factors and their insertion in the estimation equation. Alternatively, one can use a somewhat more indirect approach. Since the qualities that make a place attractive for travelers also contribute to the demand for transportation-substitutes, one should be able to deduce the measure of attractiveness from the demand for the latter. Some of the trip's closest substitutes are found among other communication activities. For example, the daily volume of intercity telephone calls depends on telephone rates, the attractiveness of the two cities, and their population size; the latter variable playing a dual role as a scale factor and as one of the factors determining the city's attractiveness. We assume that these three variables are exhaustive,

$$\log N_j = A_0 + A_1 \log P_{Tj} + A_2 \log G'_j + A_3 G''_j, \tag{5.8}$$

where N_j denotes the average daily volume of long distance calls from New York to city j ($j = 1, 2, \ldots, 38$), P_{Tj} is the corresponding telephone rate, G'_j is the population size of SMSA j, and G''_j stands for the other factors determining the attractiveness of j. Put differently, the attractiveness measure G''_j can be derived as the residual in the logarithmic regression of the dependent variable N_j on the two measurable independent variables P_{Tj} and G'_j

$$G''_j = \frac{1}{A_3} (\log N_j - A_0 - A_1 \log P_{Tj} - A_2 \log G'_j). \tag{5.9}$$

Specifically,

$$G''_j = \frac{1}{A_3} [\log N_j - (8.7979 - \underset{(.2393)}{1.6016} \log P_{Tj} + \underset{(.0937)}{1.0059} \log G'_j)]$$

$$\text{adj } R^2 = .80, \tag{5.10}$$

where the figures in parentheses represent the corresponding standard errors of the regression coefficients.[7] Assuming arbitrarily that $A_3 = 1$, we

[7] The information on the daily volume and the telephone rates (measured in cents per 3 minutes) was obtained through the courtesy of the American Telephone and Telegraph Company, Long Lines Department, New York. The information on the SMSAs' population (measured in thousands) is based on the 1960 *Census of Population,* Table 33. An alternative measure, the volume of intercity mail, had to be rejected because of the nonexistence of such data.

used as the attractiveness measure (G_j in equation 5.7) two variables: population size (G'_j) and the residual (G''_j)

$$\log X_{ij} = \beta_0 + \beta_1 \log (P_j + kW_iT_j) + \beta_2 \log Y_i \\ + \beta'_3 \log G'_j + \beta''_3 G''_j + u_{ij}. \tag{5.11}$$

Intercity telephone rates are linearly related to intercity distance. The definition of the attractiveness factor (G''_j) is based, therefore, on the tacit belief that the destination's distance does not affect its attractiveness. This is an assumption that is somewhat hard to defend in the case of business trips. More than one-third of all air passenger trips are for the purpose of visiting a customer, a branch, an agent, the home office, or the supplier.[8] In this case, the knowledge of the market and transportation and communication costs favor a place that is close at hand, and the attractiveness of a place is, therefore, inversely related to distance. The adverse effect distance has on the demand for trips may be explained in this case by its adverse effect on the attractiveness of the visit and by its direct effect on the trip's price. By ignoring the first of these two effects (assuming that the covariance between M_j and G''_j equals zero) one tends to overplay the role of the second; that is, one tends to overestimate the price effect.

The dependent variable describes the average number of trips to a given destination by travelers in a certain income group. Each such average is based on a different number of observations. To correct for heteroscedasticity due to a different number of observations in each cell, we employed a weighted regression.[9] The estimates of equation (5.11) are presented in Table 7.[10]

The explanatory power of the equation is very high both in the case of business and personal trips (the adjusted R^2 are .9 and .8, respectively). The major determinants of the demand for air travel are the traveler's skills and his place in the organizational hierarchy, as reflected by his income. Differences in income explain over one half of the dispersion of the number of trips among different individuals and among

[8] The Port of New York Authority, *op. cit.,* Table 10, p. 59.

[9] See S. J. Prais and H. S. Houthakker, *The Analysis of Family Budgets,* Cambridge, 1955, pp. 55–62.

[10] For a glossary of the terms used, see Table 8. We also tried to fit some other functional forms to the data: the linear, the semilogarithmic, and the semilogarithmic reciprocal. All these forms yielded results that were inferior to those of the simple logarithmic function.

TABLE 7

Partial Regression Coefficients of Business and Personal Trips

$$\log X = b_0 + b_1 \log (P + kWT) + b_2 \log Y + b_3 \log G' + b_4 G''$$

		Intercept		Price	
k	adj. R^2	b_0	t	b_1	t
BUSINESS TRIPS					
0	.87688	−16.63	−31.45	−.67	−15.46
A. W = Wage professionals					
.25	.88012	−17.29	−33.62	−.75	−15.98
.50	.88152	−17.82	−35.06	−.80	−16.21
.75	.88214	−18.24	−36.07	−.85	−16.32
1.00	.88238	−18.59	−36.81	−.88	−16.36
1.15[a]	.88242	−18.78	−37.15	−.90	−16.37
1.25[a]	.88242	−18.89	−37.35	−.91	−16.36
2.00	.88204	−19.57	−38.30	−.98	−16.30
B. W = Wage male professionals					
.25	.87959	−17.35	−33.68	−.75	−15.90
.50	.88039	−17.91	−35.10	−.80	−16.03
.65[a]	.88049	−18.19	−35.72	−.83	−16.04
.70[a]	.88049	−18.27	−35.89	−.84	−16.04
.75	.88047	−18.36	−36.06	−.85	−16.04
1.00	.88022	−18.73	−36.71	−.88	−16.00
2.00	.87840	−19.73	−37.91	−.98	−15.70
PERSONAL TRIPS					
0[a]	.81156	−11.23	−21.68	−.34	−7.42
A. W = Average wage					
.25	.80786	−11.52	−22.41	−.33	−6.84
.50	.80519	−11.72	−22.92	−.33	−6.41
.75	.80313	−11.87	−23.29	−.33	−6.06
1.00	.80149	−11.99	−23.58	−.32	−5.77
2.00	.79720	−12.29	−24.21	−.30	−4.96
B. W = Weighted average wage					
.25	.80936	−11.42	−22.18	−.34	−7.08
.50	.80764	−11.56	−22.55	−.34	−6.81
.75	.80623	−11.68	−22.85	−.35	−6.58
1.00	.80506	−11.77	−23.09	−.35	−6.38
2.00	.80175	−12.02	−23.69	−.35	−5.82

[a] R^2 at maximum.

Income		Population		Tastes	
b_2	t	b_3	t	b_4	t
1.80	40.49	76	19.40	.96	13.95
1.90	42.79	.77	19.85	.95	14.03
1.98	43.80	.78	20.11	.95	14.03
2.05	44.15	.78	20.27	.95	14.01
2.11	44.15	.78	20.38	.94	13.97
2.14	44.05	.79	20.43	.94	13.95
2.16	43.96	.79	20.46	.94	13.93
2.27	42.96	.80	20.60	.93	13.81
1.91	42.77	.77	19.82	.95	14.00
1.99	43.62	.78	20.02	.95	13.98
2.04	43.77	.78	20.09	.95	13.95
2.05	43.79	.78	20.11	.95	13.94
2.06	43.78	.78	20.13	.95	13.93
2.12	43.59	.78	20.19	.94	13.87
2.29	41.82	.80	20.27	.94	13.63
1.21	31.21	.52	12.26	1.31	23.21
1.24	31.58	.52	12.24	1.30	22.90
1.26	31.50	.53	12.21	1.30	22.67
1.28	31.22	.53	12.19	1.29	22.50
1.29	30.84	.53	12.18	1.29	22.36
1.32	29.06	.53	12.12	1.28	22.00
1.23	31.57	.52	12.27	1.31	23.04
1.25	31.67	.53	12.28	1.31	22.91
1.26	31.62	.53	12.28	1.30	22.80
1.28	31.48	.53	12.28	1.30	22.70
1.31	30.56	.53	12.27	1.30	22.43

TABLE 8

Glossary of Symbols and Notations

Notation	Name	Explanation	Unit
X_{ij}	Trips per family	Number of trips to destination j per family in income group i	Trips per thousand families per year
G'_j	Population	The population size of the SMSA of destination j	Thousands
G''_j	Tastes	The residual of the logarithmic regression of number of telephone calls on telephone rates and population	
Y_i	Income	Average income for income group i	Dollars per annum
P_j	Fare	Airline average economy fare from New York to destination j	Dollars
T_j	Elapsed time	Elapsed traveling time (based on the fastest flying time to destination j)	Hours
K_i	Price of time	The value the traveler places on his time	Dollars per hour
Π_{ij}	Price of the trip	$= P_j + K_i T_j$	Dollars
W_i	Hourly earnings	Average of hourly earning of managers and professionals (or male managers and professionals)	Dollars per hour
k	The ratio of the price of time to hourly earnings	$= K_i / W_i$	

different places, price playing only a minor role in the explanation of traffic patterns. The absolute value of the income and price elasticities was found to be higher in the case of business trips than in the case of personal trips. In both cases the income elasticities (2.0 and 1.2) are significantly greater than unity, and the price elasticities ($-.8$ and $-.3$) are smaller than one. (In the case of business trips this result is not statistically significant at a level of significance of $\alpha = .01$.)

The effect income has on personal trips differs conceptually from the effect it has on business trips. For personal trips income measures the **passenger's ability to pay** for the trip, while for business trips it is a proxy for the passenger's skills and, hence, the difference between his marginal product at the point of origin and at the point of destination. A comparison of the income elasticities is, therefore, meaningless.

The finding that business travelers are more sensitive than personal travelers to changes in the trip's price may at first seem somewhat surprising. This difference may be explained by differences in the frequency and the duration of the trip, and by biases resulting from an inaccurate measurement of the attractiveness factor. The average frequency of air trips of a business traveler is more than twice as large as that of a personal traveler (8 trips vs. 3 trips per year, respectively).[11] The rate of return and the investment in information are, therefore, going to be greater in the case of business trips than in the case of personal trips. This increased investment in information increases the business traveler's sensitivity to change in price. Alternatively, this difference may be explained by the smaller share of the trip's price in the cost of the visit. The costs of the visit vary directly with its duration. The duration of a business visit is significantly shorter than the duration of a personal trip. Business trips constitute over 75 per cent of all visits with a duration of three nights or less, but accounted for less than 40 per cent of the trips that lasted eight nights or more.[12] A percentage increase in the trip's price increases the costs of a personal visit less than the costs of a business visit, and results in an increased price elasticity for business trips. Finally, it was shown that the estimates of the price elasticity of business trips may suffer from an upward bias originating in the assumption that the attractiveness measure (G''_j) and distance are uncorrelated.[13]

We were unable to derive an estimate of the value placed on time by personal travelers. On the other hand, for business travelers we estimated that the price of time almost equals hourly earnings. In investigating the demand for personal trips, equation (5.11) assumes its highest explanatory power when the price of time is assumed to equal zero. On the other hand, in the case of business trips, R^2 is at its maximum when $1.15 < k < 1.25$ when the price of time is related to the hourly earning of professionals and managers, and at $.65 < k < .70$ when the price of time is related to the wage of male professionals and managers. Both of

[11] The Port of New York Authority, *op. cit.*, p. 24.
[12] *Ibid.*, p. 17.
[13] See p. 46 above.

these values do not differ significantly from the explanatory value of the equation when $k = 1.0$, i.e., both estimates are consistent with the hypothesis that the price of time equals hourly earnings. On the other hand, both equations yield a significantly higher explanatory value than the assumption $k = 0$, i.e., the assumption that the price of time is unrelated to income. The omission of the cost of time effect results, as Table 7 clearly indicates, in an underestimate of both the price and the income elasticities.[14] Note, however, that k is a random variable and subject to a random distribution, and may also admit, therefore, some different interpretations.

The results concerning personal trips prove again to be puzzling. The finding that the price of time is unrelated to hourly earnings can be explained only in terms of the low degree of substitution of time between work and nonwork activities. Of all personal trips, over one half were taken during a weekend or a holiday, and almost one half were taken by travelers who were unemployed (the corresponding figures for business trips were 39 and 4 per cent respectively).[15] The

[14] Compare the estimated parameters of business trips when $k = 0$ and when $k = 1.25$ These results support the theoretical expectations: let the true relationship be

$$y = \beta_1 x_1 + \beta_2 z + u;$$

a misspecification results in an estimate,

$$y = b_1 x_1 + b_2 x_2 + e;$$

then

$$Eb_1 = \beta_1 + \beta_2 \gamma_{zx_1 \cdot x_2},$$

and

$$Eb_2 = \beta_2 \gamma_{zx_2 \cdot x_1},$$

where $\gamma_{zx_1 \cdot x_2}$ denotes the partial regression coefficient of z on x_1 holding x_2 constant.

In our specific case

$$z = \log (P + kWT),$$
$$x_1 = \log Y,$$

and

$$x_2 = \log P.$$

Hence, $\gamma_{zx_1 \cdot x_2} > 0$, $\gamma_{zx_2 \cdot x_1} < 1$, and $\beta_2 < 0$. Consequently,

$$E(b_1) < \beta_1, |E(b_2)| < |\beta_2|.$$

[15] The Port of New York Authority, *op. cit.*, pp. 18, 50, 76.

foregone earnings involved in these personal trips are substantially lower than those involved in business trips taken on a regular weekday. Still, these differences may not explain the complete lack of responsiveness to the amount of elapsed time. The estimation of the price of time of personal travelers calls for additional investigation.

To test our assumption that the price of time is not affected by distance we reestimated the demand for business trips, limiting our observations to routes whose distance exceeds 175 miles. An estimate of equation (5.11) based on 35 city pairs is reported in Table 9. The experiment was repeated for business trips to the 23 cities whose distance from New York exceeds 500 miles.

Equation (5.11) attains its maximum explanatory power in the first case when $.95 < k < 1.05$ and in the second case when $1.15 < k < 1.20$ (see Table 9). The price elasticity in both cases is somewhat (though not significantly) smaller than unity ($.9 < \hat{\beta}_1 < 1.0$) and the income elasticity is significantly greater than one ($\hat{\beta}_2 = 2.1$). The comparison of these results with the results of Table 7 does not indicate any systematic relationship between the price of time and distance.

Past studies have argued that the New York demand for air trips differs from that of other cities.[16] The Port of New York Authority data does not allow for a direct test of this hypothesis. An indirect test of the hypothesis is based on the comparison of the demand of New York residents leaving the city and the demand of residents of other places going home. The estimates of (5.11) for resident business travelers are reported in Table 10.

The estimates tend to confirm our previous findings that the price elasticity of business trips is close to unity, the income elasticity is close to two, and the price of time of business travelers equals their hourly earnings. We could not find any evidence substantiating the claim that these results are peculiar to New York City.

How do these estimates compare with existing estimates of the price and income elasticities and with some implicit estimates of k? There are hardly two studies in this field that agree on the values of the income and price elasticities. The argument whether the price elasticity, a crucial variable for any pricing policy, is less or greater than unity goes back

[16] J. B. Lansing, Jung Chao Liu, and D. B. Suits, "An Analysis of Interurban Air Travel," *Quarterly Journal of Economics*, February 1961.

TABLE 9

Partial Regression Coefficients of Business Trips by Distance

$$[\log X = b_0 + b_1 \log (P + kWT) + b_2 \log Y + b_3 \log G' + b_4 G'']$$

		Intercept		Price	
k	adj. R^2	b_0	t	b_1	t

175 + MILES

A. W = Wage professionals

.25	.89243	−16.94	−33.41	−.81	−17.47
.50	.89370	−17.49	−34.99	−.87	−17.69
.75	.89417	−17.95	−36.11	−.92	−17.77
.95[a]	.89427	−18.26	−36.77	−.95	−17.79
1.00[a]	.89427	−18.33	−36.91	−.96	−17.79
1.05[a]	.89427	−18.39	−37.05	−.96	−17.79
2.00	.89348	−19.37	−38.59	−1.06	−17.65

B. W = Wage male professionals

.25	.89184	−17.00	−33.47	−.82	−17.37
.50	.89247	−17.59	−35.02	−.87	−17.47
.55[a]	.89248	−17.70	−35.26	−.88	−17.48
.60[a]	.89248	−17.80	−35.49	−.89	−17.48
.75	.89236	−18.07	−36.07	−.92	−17.45
1.00	.89194	−18.47	−36.80	−.95	−17.38
2.00	.88957	−19.55	−38.14	−1.06	−16.98

500 + MILES

A. W = Wage professionals

.25	.88843	−17.17	−26.47	−.75	−8.42
.50	.88946	−17.55	−27.98	−.80	−8.59
.75	.88998	−17.89	−29.20	−.83	−8.67
1.00	.89019	−18.19	−30.18	−.86	−8.70
1.15[a]	.89023	−18.35	−30.67	−.87	−8.71
1.20[a]	.89023	−18.40	−30.82	−.88	−8.71
2.00	.88981	−19.07	−32.46	−.93	−8.64

B. W = Wage male professionals

.25	.88805	−17.22	−26.58	−.75	−8.37
.50	.88872	−17.64	−28.15	−.79	−8.47
.70[a]	.88885	−17.93	−29.16	−.82	−8.49
.75[a]	.88885	−18.00	−29.38	−.83	−8.49
1.00	.88872	−18.32	−30.35	−.85	−8.47
2.00	.88725	−19.24	−32.44	−.91	−8.24

[a]R^2 at maximum.

Income		Population		Tastes	
b_2	t	b_3	t	b_4	t
1.91	43.93	.75	19.64	.89	13.29
2.00	45.03	.75	19.92	.88	13.30
2.07	45.42	.76	20.09	.88	13.27
2.12	45.45	.76	20.19	.88	13.24
2.13	45.44	.76	20.21	.88	13.23
2.14	45.41	.77	20.23	.88	13.22
2.31	44.21	.78	20.44	.87	13.05
1.92	43.90	.75	19.60	.89	13.26
2.01	44.82	.76	19.82	.88	13.24
2.02	44.90	.76	19.85	.88	13.23
2.04	44.95	.76	19.87	.88	13.22
2.08	45.00	.76	19.94	.88	13.18
2.15	44.80	.77	20.00	.88	13.12
2.33	42.93	.78	20.08	.87	12.86
1.90	35.22	.76	20.07	.72	8.77
1.96	35.42	.77	20.28	.71	8.73
2.02	35.11	.77	20.43	.71	8.68
2.07	34.56	.78	20.52	.70	8.64
2.09	34.17	.78	20.57	.70	8.61
2.10	34.04	.78	20.58	.70	8.60
2.21	21.90	.79	20.69	.70	8.48
1.91	35.18	.76	20.04	.72	8.76
1.97	35.22	.77	20.22	.71	8.70
2.02	34.86	.77	20.31	.71	8.65
2.03	34.73	.77	20.33	.71	8.64
2.08	34.00	.78	20.39	.71	8.59
2.22	30.84	.79	20.43	.70	8.40

TABLE 10

Partial Regression Coefficients of Business Trips by New York Residents

$$[\log X = b_0 + b_1 \log (P + kWT) + b_2 \log Y + b_3 \log G' + b_4 G'']$$

		Intercept		Price	
k	adj. R^2	b_0	t	b_1	t
0	.83409	−18.07	−28.95	−.64	−12.78
A. W = Wage professionals					
.25	.83732	−18.69	−30.68	−.72	−13.19
.50	.83869	−19.19	−31.84	−.77	−13.37
.75	.83925	−19.60	−32.66	−.81	−13.44
1.00[a]	.83940	−19.94	−33.25	−.85	−13.46
1.10[a]	.83940	−20.06	−33.43	−.86	−13.46
2.00	.83855	−20.88	−34.42	−.94	−13.35
B. W = Wage male professionals					
.25	.83690	−18.74	−30.74	−.72	−13.14
.50	.83778	−19.27	−31.91	−.77	−13.25
.65[a]	.83789	−19.54	−32.42	−.80	−13.26
.70[a]	.83789	−19.62	−32.56	−.81	−13.26
.75	.83787	−19.70	−32.70	−.82	−13.26
1.00	.83762	−20.06	−33.25	−.85	−13.23
2.00	.83552	−21.03	−34.24	−.94	−12.96

[a] R^2 at maximum.

into the fifties and has not yet been resolved.[17] The same dispersion is found in estimates of the income elasticity. The results prove to be very sensitive to the source of data used (time series vs. cross-sections), the independent variables included in the equation, and the equation's functional form. Any comparison made among the various estimates becomes, under these circumstances, meaningless.

Alternatively, one could evaluate the reliability of the different estimates by comparing their performance as predictors. However, most of the studies in the field are of quite recent origin and use up-to-date data. Their predictive power is not yet known and will not be for many years to come.

[17] For a summary of some of the arguments, see R. Caves, *Air Transport and Its Regulators,* Cambridge, Massachusetts, 1962, Ch. 2, pp. 34–54.

Income		Population		Tastes	
b_2	t	b_3	t	b_4	t
1.77	33.71	.91	20.36	.86	12.77
1.86	35.40	.92	20.72	.85	12.79
1.94	36.13	.92	20.92	.84	12.76
2.01	36.37	.93	21.05	.84	12.70
2.06	36.34	.93	21.13	.83	12.63
2.08	36.28	.93	21.16	.83	12.60
2.22	35.29	.94	21.30	.82	12.33
1.87	35.41	.92	20.69	.85	12.77
1.95	36.06	.92	20.87	.84	12.72
1.99	36.17	.93	20.93	.84	12.67
2.01	36.18	.93	20.95	.84	12.65
2.02	36.17	.93	20.96	.84	12.64
2.08	36.02	.93	21.02	.83	12.55
2.24	34.59	.95	21.10	.82	12.21

There are at least four published studies that attempt to estimate the trade-off between time and money in transportation. One of these studies, Blackburn's study of traveling patterns in California,[18] employs a functional form that does not allow an easy comparison of his results with ours. Becker estimated the value of time from the relation between the value of land and the commuting distance from home to place of employment. An estimate based on the experience of commuters in Seattle rendered a value of time which was about 40 per cent of the commuter's average hourly earning.[19] The third study is based on the

[18] A. J. Blackburn, "A Nonlinear Model of Passenger Demand," in *Studies in Travel Demand*, Vol. II, prepared by Mathematica for the Department of Transportation, Princeton, New Jersey, 1966.

[19] Gary S. Becker, "A Theory of the Allocation of Time," *Economic Journal*, September 1965, p. 510.

commuter's experience in London. Beesley tried to estimate what is essentially the switching distance between the various modes of public transportation. Given these estimates, he then estimated the price of time of two different income groups, observing a value of time which was 30–35 per cent of the hourly wage.[20] The difference between these estimates and our estimate of the business traveler's price of time can be attributed to the peculiar nature of commutation trips. Commutation can be regarded as "productive consumption." It is a consumption activity that serves as an input in the production of the activity "work." As shown in Chapter 2, the value of time in such activity equals the wage rate only if the traveler is free to substitute working time for traveling time and if work does not yield any disutility. If either of these two assumptions is violated we may expect the price of time to be lower than the wage rate.

The fourth and most recent of these studies is the forecast by the Institute for Defense Analyses of the future demand for trips by supersonic passenger planes. This study concludes "that passengers in the aggregate act as though they value their time at approximately their earning rate," and that there is no evidence that personal travelers differ in that respect from business travelers.[21] We cannot agree with the second finding, but the IDA's aggregate estimates fully support our findings with respect to the price of time of business travelers.

[20] M. E. Beesley, "The Value of Time Spent in Traveling: Some New Evidence," *Economica,* May 1965.

[21] Institute for Defense Analyses, *Demand Analysis of Air Travel by Supersonic Transport,* Washington, D.C., December 1966, Vol. I, pp. xv, 16–19; Vol. II, Appendix C, pp. 31–59.

SIX

Some Applications

THIS STUDY of the effect of time on the demand for passenger transportation would be incomplete without returning to the opening thesis, i.e., the claim that the theory of the allocation of time provides the analyst with a powerful tool for the estimation of the demand for some of the future modes of transportation. We mentioned several of these modes in the introduction, the supersonic passenger plane (SST), the high-speed train, the short-take-off plane (STOL), and the vertical-take-off plane (VTOL). The precise evaluation of the demand for these modes is clearly outside the scope of this study. It involves a vast amount of data, of which some is still confidential, some in dispute, and some unresolved from the technological point of view. Thus, we will limit ourselves to hypothetical case studies.

The introduction of new modes provides the traveler with a new, hitherto nonexisting, combination of time and money inputs, and it cuts into the market of the existing modes. Let the new mode (say, mode S) be faster than any existing mode. Let the previously fastest mode be mode A. Given the new mode's fare and traveling time on a specific route (P_S and T_S, respectively), all mode A travelers whose price of time exceeds

$$K > \frac{P_S - P_A}{T_A - T_S} = K^*_{S-A} \qquad (6.1)$$

will shift to the new mode. The new mode (or the new equipment) should be able to capture the entire mode A market if the price of time for all passengers exceeds K^*_{S-A} (a sufficient condition being $P_S < P_A$).[1]

---

[1] We still maintain that the choice of mode rests solely on traveling costs, ignoring other factors affecting the utility derived from the trip, such as prestige, risk, etc.

FIGURE 5

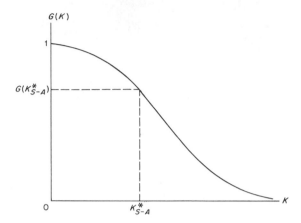

Otherwise, the market will split between the conventional and the new mode. Given the mode A travelers' decreasing cumulative distribution of the price of time $G(K)$ (i.e., the distribution describing the percentage of travelers with a price of time exceeding K), $G(K^*_{S-A})$ of all travelers will shift to the new mode (see Figure 5). This percentage depends on the precise value of K^*_{S-A} and on the shape of $G(K)$.

To illustrate, assume a supersonic plane, whose cruising speed is 1,500 mph, is to be introduced in 1975.[2] Should the new equipment prove to be cheaper to operate than conventional equipment (including the new jumbo-jets), and should the air carriers decide to charge for the use of the new equipment the same or lower fare than that charged for the old mode, the SST should have no difficulties in wresting from the subsonic plane the whole market in which it will operate. If, on the other hand, the air carriers decide to impose a surcharge for the use of the new plane, the market will be split between the two sorts of equipment. In this case one has not only to estimate the size of the air travel market in the mid-seventies but also the share of each kind of equipment in this market.

Addressing ourselves to the second task, we assume that the new equipment does not affect the fixed component of the trip's elapsed

---

[2] We ignore any possible imposition of speed restrictions on overland flights to limit the effects of sonic booms.

time, and that the introduction of the jumbo-jet will not change the elapsed time and the fare of conventional equipment. Given our estimates of Chapter 4 [equation (4.1)], and a percentage surcharge on the new equipment at a rate of q, the elapsed time and pecuniary costs of subsonic and supersonic planes are

$$T_A = 2.56 + .00210M, \qquad P_A = 7.04 + .06006M,$$
$$T_S = 2.56 + .00067M, \text{ and } \quad P_A = (1 + q)(7.04 + .06006M), \qquad (6.2)$$

respectively, where the elapsed time (T_i) is measured in hours, the fare (P_i) in dollars, and the distance (M) in miles. The traveler uses the faster mode only if his price of time exceeds

$$K > q\left(42.00 + \frac{4908.8}{M}\right) = K^*_{S-A}, \qquad (6.3)$$

where K^*_{S-A} is measured in dollars per hour.

The proposed supersonic plane cannot compete with conventional equipment for the short-range trips. The unit operating costs of the new equipment decrease with distance relative to those of conventional equipment and it will not be operated for distances smaller than 700 miles. For a range exceeding 700 miles the critical value of K^*_{S-A} becomes almost insensitive to changes in distance. Thus, given a surcharge of 10 per cent ($q = .1$), the value of K^* ranges from $4.40 to $4.80 per hour. Assuming a surcharge of 20 or 50 per cent these values are about $9.50 and $23.00 per hour, respectively (see Table 11 and Chart 5). Imposing a surcharge of 10 per cent, the SST will be used only by passengers whose price of time exceeds $4.20 per hour. Raising the surcharge to 20 or 50 per cent limits the SST's clientele to travelers who place on their time a value exceeding $8.40 and $21.00 per hour, respectively.

The distribution of the price of time that will face the SST in 1975 depends on the future distribution of earnings and the relationship between the price of time and hourly earnings. Adopting the income distribution of air traveler-trips as reported in the Port of New York Authority survey (Table 12 and Chart 6), we estimated the corresponding distribution of hourly earnings using the 1/1,000 sample of the 1960 Census of Population data on the hourly earnings of professionals and managers (see Table 6). To obtain the 1975 distribution of hourly earnings we assumed that the hourly earnings of all travelers increase at the

TABLE 11

The Critical Value of Time Determining the Choice Between Supersonic and Conventional Equipment

$$(K_{S-A}^* = q[42.00 + (4908.8/M)])$$

Distance M (miles)	K_{S-A}^*/q (dollars per hour)	K_{S-A}^*		
		$q = .1$	$q = .2$	$q = .5$
250	61.63	6.16	12.33	30.82
500	51.82	5.18	10.36	25.91
750	48.54	4.85	9.71	24.27
1,000	46.91	4.69	9.38	23.46
1,250	45.93	4.59	9.19	22.97
1,500	45.27	4.53	9.05	22.64
1,750	44.80	4.48	8.96	22.40
2,000	44.45	4.45	8.89	22.23
2,250	44.18	4.42	8.84	22.09
2,500	43.96	4.40	8.79	21.98
∞	42.00	4.20	8.40	21.00

constant rate of about 3 per cent per annum (i.e., an increase of 40 per cent for the period 1963–75). Finally, we assume that this distribution (see Chart 7) does not change with distance.[3]

The SST's share of the market depends on the value of K_{S-A}^* and the distribution of the price of time, $G(K)$. Given the information above, this share is a function of two parameters: the surcharge rate (q) and the ratio of the price of time to hourly earnings (k).

To isolate the effect of changes in the SST's surcharge, let us assume that air travelers place on their time a value equal to their hourly earnings (the effect of this assumption is to be examined later). Fixing the surcharge at a rate of 10 per cent discourages all air travelers with a price of time of less than about \$4.50 per hour from using the new plane. Given these hypothetical assumptions, SST travelers would constitute over 80 per cent of all traveler-trips. Any increase in the surcharge

[3] This assumption would be grossly oversimplified were all distance ranges to be concerned. It may serve as a better approximation when one concentrates on the range beyond 700 miles.

CHART 5

The Critical Value of Time Determining the Choice Between Supersonic and Conventional Equipment

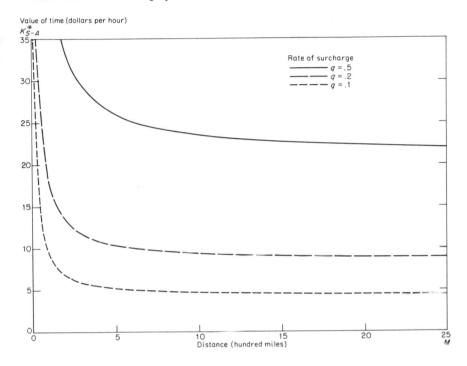

Value of time (dollars per hour)

K^*_{S-A}

Rate of surcharge
———— $q = .5$
— — — $q = .2$
- - - - $q = .1$

Distance (hundred miles)

cuts into the attractiveness of the new mode. Thus, raising the surcharge to 20 per cent ($K^* = \$9.50$ per hour), the SST's share drops to 35 per cent, and imposing a surcharge of 50 per cent ($K^* = \$23.00$ per hour) leaves the new plane with less than 10 per cent of the market.

About one-third of all air passengers and about two-thirds of all passenger miles in 1964 were to a distance exceeding 700 miles.[4] We assume that the distribution of air travelers by distance of trip will not change over the next decade. Thus, given our illustrative assumptions, with a surcharge of 10 per cent the supersonic plane will be able to capture close to 30 per cent of all air travelers and over 55 per cent of

[4] Civil Aeronautics Board, *Handbook of Airline Statistics, 1965 Edition*, Washington, D.C., December 1965, p. 406.

TABLE 12

Distribution of Income of Air Travelers: 1963

Annual Family Income All Incomes (dollars)	Per Cent	Cumulative Percentage
Under 5,000	5.0	100.0
5,000— 5,999	3.2	95.0
6,000— 6,999	3.7	91.8
7,000— 9,999	11.0	88.1
10,000—10,999	8.0	77.1
11,000—14,999	17.4	69.1
15,000—19,999	16.4	51.7
20,000—24,999	9.6	35.3
25,000 and over	25.7	25.7

SOURCE: *Port of New York Authority Survey*, 38 most heavily trafficked routes.

CHART 6

Distribution of Income of Air Traveler-Trips: 1963

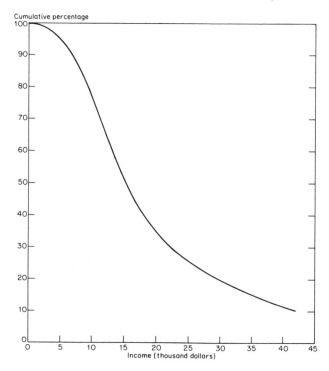

CHART 7

Estimated Distribution of Hourly Earnings of Air Traveler-Trips: 1975

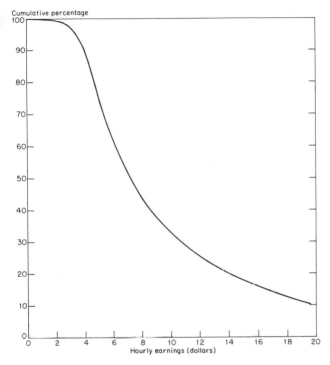

all passenger miles. Doubling the surcharge to 20 per cent, these shares shrink to a little over 10 and 25 per cent, respectively.

The share of travelers switching to the new equipment proves to be very sensitive to changes in the surcharge rate. The same applies to changes in the assumptions on the value the passengers assign to their time. Given a surcharge of 10 per cent and assuming that the passengers value their time at a rate equal to their hourly earnings, we found that over 80 per cent of all long range passenger trips will switch to the SST. Had we assumed that the passengers place on their time a value that is only one half of their hourly earnings, we should have concluded that this share will be cut to about 35 per cent of the market (this assumption having the same effect as that of a surcharge of 20 per cent, where the price of time equals hourly earnings). On the other hand, if the travelers value their time, as some airlines believe, at twice their wage rate [5] the new equipment should be able to squeeze the old one out of the long-range market almost entirely (the SST's share exceeding 95 per cent). Moreover, even an increase in the surcharge rate to 20 per cent would not impair, in this case, the SST's dominance, the SST still being able to maintain over 80 per cent of the market.

We pointed out in Chapter 4 some of the difficulties the railroads face competing with the bus and air carriers in the passenger transportation market. Problems of scheduling, lack of divisibility, and increasingly dispersed origins and destinations hamper the railroads in their rivalry with the other modes of transportation. It was suggested that one way to overcome these handicaps would be to increase the trains' speed.

In Chapter 4 we assumed that there are no costs or time involved in reaching or leaving the railroad station, and, hence, traveling by train involves no fixed time component. The effective marginal speed of the trains was found to be 40 mph, where the distance is measured in terms of city-center-to-city-center great-circle statute miles. The low effective speed is explained by a low cruising speed, a great number of stops, and circuity.[6]

These estimates of a train trip's elapsed time, though high, give the railroads a credit they do not deserve. The assumption that a trip by train does not involve any fixed time component is bold, at best. Traveling to and from the stations does take time. Moreover, infrequent train schedules result in a fixed component of waiting time. This component may be considerable, and it is increasing as the frequency of train departures falls. Any attempt to cut the elapsed time of a trip by train has, therefore, to concentrate on increasing the frequency of trains and their cruising speed and decreasing the number and length of stops.

The fixed time component of air trips is about 2.5 hours [see equation

[5] Institute for Defense Analyses, *Demand Analysis for Air Travel by Supersonic Transport,* Washington, D.C., December 1966, Vol. II, p. 53.

[6] The traveling distance between any two city-pairs by rail was found in the Washington-Boston Corridor to be about 20 per cent greater than that of a plane. See System Analysis and Research Corporation, *Demand for Intercity Passenger Travel in the Washington-Boston Corridor,* Boston, Massachusetts. This estimate may be too high for some areas (e.g., more sparsely populated areas) and too low for others (e.g., mountainous terrain).

(4.1), p. 25].[7] Let us assume that the railroads are able to modify their schedules so as to maintain a one hour edge over the air carriers (i.e., $\alpha_{OA} - \alpha_{OR} = 1$ hour), and are able to increase their cruising speed and cut the number of stops so as to increase their marginal effective speed to:

    a. 100 mph (i.e., $\alpha_{IR} = 0.0100$),
    b. 150 mph (i.e., $\alpha_{IR} = 0.0067$), and
    c. 300 mph (i.e., $\alpha_{IR} = 0.0033$).[8]

In order to predict the effect of the introduction of these new modes on the modal split one has to know the increase in fares associated with the increased speed, and the distribution of the travelers' price of time (or alternatively, the travelers' income) by distance traveled and by mode used. In the absence of these data we will have to revert to some hypothetical calculations of the point at which air carriers will enter into the market.

A plane cruising at a speed of 500 mph overtakes a train that departed one hour earlier and that travels at a speed of 100 mph after traveling only 125 miles. Had the train been traveling at a speed of 150 mph this distance would have been 214 miles, and had the speed been 300 mph the distance would have been 750 miles. Under our illustrative example, the railroads will almost have to quadruple their effective speed in order to recoup the 200 mile range market, and, in particular, the most lucrative routes of the Northcastern corridor.[9] Only an eightfold increase in

---

[7] This fixed time component consists of traveling to and from the airport, waiting time, and a fixed time component associated with take-off and landing. The above estimate may have an upward bias because it is based on traveling time to the airport by limousine and because the origin of all flights is New York. This bias may be offset by our failure to account for waiting time due to infrequent flights.

[8] These assumptions are quite far reaching. If one takes account of the circuity factor (say, 1.2), then to satisfy these requirements a nonstop train would have to travel at speeds of (a) 120 mph, (b) 180 mph, and (c) 360 mph, respectively. The last of these alternatives resembles a short-take-off or a vertical-take-off plane more than any known form of ground transportation.

[9] The distances of the two most popular air routes, New York–Boston and New York–Washington, are 188 and 205 miles, respectively. Among the Northeast corridor's major routes only Boston-Washington and Boston-Philadelphia exceed 214 miles.

The statement, of course, takes an extreme view. Even more modest increases in the train's speed may increase the railroad's share of this market.

the railroads' speed will insure them of the medium range market. A speed of 300 mph may well be outside the train's reach, befitting more a STOL or VTOL plane. The introduction of these new aircrafts may cost, therefore, the conventional airline equipment over two-thirds of air passengers and one-third of air passenger miles.

The train should be better off if it succeeds in improving schedule frequency further so as to give it a two hour edge over the plane (i.e., $\alpha_{OA} - \alpha_{OR} = 2$ hours). In this case, even a 100 mph train should be able to recapture the short range distance (the plane overtaking the train only after 250 miles). Moreover, a 500 mph subsonic plane competing with a 300 mph train, VTOL, or STOL plane has to travel 1,500 miles before it overcomes the two hour handicap. This leaves the slower mode with most of the domestic market except for the transcontinental routes.

One can indulge in this kind of speculation indefinitely. Unfortunately, this kind of analysis suffers from one major drawback. It ignores any changes in the railroads' operating costs and in their fare. The conclusions in the previous section are based on the tacit assumption that in spite of any possible increase in fare the train will still be able to provide the traveler with a cheaper service (in pecuniary terms) than the air carriers. Given the 1963 pecuniary charges [equation (4.1)], the air carriers' charges exceed those of the train by about 40 per cent.[10] The train should, therefore, be able to recuperate the above mentioned gains from the increased speed only if it succeeds in keeping its fares at a level that is less than 1.4 times their current level. This margin is all the tighter since railroads in the U.S. generally lose considerable sums on their passenger traffic at the current tariff level while airlines have been modestly profitable.

---

[10] Our estimate in Chapter 4 of the train trip's pecuniary cost (P_R) is biased downward as it ignores costs incurred en route (e.g., meals, sleeping accommodations, etc.). However, the extent of this bias should diminish as the train's speed is increased.

BIBLIOGRAPHY

A. BOOKS

Caves, Richard E., *Air Transport and Its Regulators,* Cambridge, Massachusetts, 1962.

Finney, D. J., *Probit Analysis,* Cambridge, England, 2nd ed., 1952.

Fisher, Franklin M., *A Priori Information and Time Series Analysis,* Amsterdam, 1962.

Fuchs, Victor R., *Differentials in Hourly Earnings by Region and City Size, 1959,* Occasional Paper 101, National Bureau of Economic Research, New York, 1967.

Houthakker, H. S., and Taylor, L. D., *Consumer Demand in the United States 1929–1970,* Cambridge, Massachusetts, 1966.

Johnston, J., *Econometric Methods,* New York, 1963.

Lansing, J. D., and Blood, D. M , *The Changing Travel Market,* Ann Arbor, Michigan, 1964.

——, *Mode Choice in Intercity Travel: A Multivariate Statistical Analysis,* Ann Arbor, Michigan, 1964.

Prais, J. S., and Houthakker, H. S., *The Analysis of Family Budgets,* Cambridge, England, 1955.

Richmond, Samuel B., *Regulation and Competition in Air Transportation,* New York, 1961.

Warner, Stanley L., *Stochastic Choice of Mode in Urban Travel: A Study in Binary Choice,* Evanston, Illinois, 1962.

B. PAPERS AND ARTICLES

Becker, Gary S., "A Theory of the Allocation of Time," *Economic Journal,* September 1965.

Beesley, M. E., "The Value of Time Spent in Traveling: Some New Evidence," *Economica,* May 1965.

Blackburn, A. J., "A Nonlinear Model of Passenger Demand," in *Studies in Travel Demand,* Vol. II, Mathematica, Princeton, New Jersey, 1966.

Brown, Samuel L., "Measuring the Elasticities of Air Travel," presented at the 125th Annual Meeting of the American Statistical Association, September 1965.

Farrar, D. E., and Glauber, P. E., "Multicollinearity in Regression Analysis: The Problem Revisited," *Review of Economics and Statistics*, February 1967.

Haavelmo, Trygve, "Remarks on Frisch's Confluence Analysis and Its Use in Econometrics," in T. Koopman, ed., *Statistical Inference in Dynamic Economic Models*, New York, 1950.

Hotelling, H., "Selection of Variates for Use in Prediction with Some Comments on the Problems of Nuisance Parameters," *Annals of Mathematical Statistics*, September 1940.

Johnson, Bruce M., "Travel Time and the Price of Leisure," *Western Economic Journal*, Spring 1966.

Joung Pyo Joun, "The Demand for Air Travel," unpublished Ph.D. dissertation, University of Washington, 1966.

Lansing, J. B., and Blood, D. M., "A Cross-Section Analysis of Non-Business Air Travel," *Journal of the American Statistical Association*, December 1958.

Lansing, J. B., Jung Chao Liu, and Suits, D. B., "An Analysis of Interurban Air Travel," *Quarterly Journal of Economics*, February 1961.

Lansing, J. B., and Neil, H. E., Jr., "An Analysis of Non-Business Rail Travel," *Land Economics*, May 1959.

Mincer, Jacob, "Market Prices, Opportunity Costs, and Income Effects" in C. F. Christ, ed., *Measurement in Economics: Studies in Mathematical Economics and Econometrics in Memory of Yehuda Grunfeld*, Stanford, California, 1963.

Moses, L. N., and Williamson, H. F., Jr., "Value of Time, Choice of Mode, and the Subsidy Issue in Urban Transportation," *Journal of Political Economy*, June 1963.

Richmond, Samuel B., "Interspatial Relationships Affecting Air Travel," *Land Economics*, February 1957.

Rybczynski, T. M., "Factor Endowment and Relative Commodity Prices," *Economica*, November 1955.

Sheshinski, Eytan, "Estimates of Demand for Air Passengers Transport: Boston–New York 1946–62," unpublished.

Tobin, James, *The Application of Multivariate Probit Analysis to Economic Survey Data*, Cowles Foundation Discussion Paper No. 1, December 1955.

C. REPORTS

American Automobile Association, "Your Driving Costs."

Bureau of the Census, *1960 Census of Population*.

——, *Census of Transportation, 1963*, Vol. I, *Passenger Transportation Survey*, Washington, D.C., 1966.

Civil Aeronautics Board, *Forecast of Airline Passenger Traffic in the United States: 1959–1965*, Washington, D.C., December 1959.

——, *Forecast of Passenger Traffic of the Domestic Trunk Air Carriers, Domestic Operations, Scheduled Service, 1965–1975*, Washington, D.C., September 1965.

——, *Handbook of Airline Statistics, 1965 Edition*, Washington, D.C., December 1965.

——, *Measuring the Elasticity of Air Passenger Demand: A Study of Changes over Time from 1953 to 1964*, Washington, D.C., February 1966.

Institute for Defense Analyses, *Demand Analysis for Air Travel by Supersonic Transport*, Washington, D.C., December 1966.

Mathematica, *Studies in Travel Demand*, Vol. II, Princeton, New Jersey, September 1966.

Opinion Research Corporation, *The Domestic Travel Market*, Princeton, New Jersey, July 1962.

The Port of New York Authority, *New York's Domestic Air Passenger Market, April 1963 through March 1964*, New York, May 1965.

——, *New York's Domestic Air Travelers, November 1955 through October 1956*, New York, October 1957.

System Analysis and Research Corporation, *Demand for Intercity Passenger Travel in the Washington-Boston Corridor*, Boston, Massachusetts.

——, *Feasibility of Developing Dollar Volumes for Increments of Time Saved by Air Travelers*, Boston, Massachusetts, February 1966.

U.S. Department of Commerce, *Approaches to the Modal Split: Intercity Transportation*, Washington, D.C., February 1967.

D. OTHER SOURCES

Fortune Magazine, November 1965, July 1966, and February 1967.

Letters from the Greyhound and Trailways bus companies, the New York Central and the Pennsylvania railroad companies, the American Automobile Association, and the American Telephone and Telegraph Company.

Russel's Official National Motorcoach Guide, 1963.

New York Times, 1965–1967.

The Official Guide of the Railways, 1963.

The Quick Reference Official Airline Guide, 1963.

INDEX